Surprised by Canon Law, Volume 2

Surprised by Canon Law, Volume 2
More Questions Catholics Ask About Canon Law

Pete Vere, J.C.L., and Michael Trueman, J.C.L.

PUBLISHED BY ST. ANTHONY MESSENGER PRESS
CINCINNATI, OHIO

RESCRIPT

In accord with the *Code of Canon Law*, I hereby grant my permission to publish *Surprised by Canon Law, Volume 2 by* Pete Vere and Michael Trueman.

Adam Cardinal Maida
Archbishop of Detroit
Detroit, Michigan
September 21, 2007

The permission to publish is a declaration that a book or pamphlet is considered to be free from doctrinal or moral error. It is not implied that those who have granted the permission to publish agree with the contents, opinions or statements expressed.

Cover design by Steve Eames
Cover photo © Dreamstime.com / Jason Signalness
Book design by Mark Sullivan

LIBRARY OF CONGRESS CATALOGING-IN-PUBLICATION DATA
Vere, Pete.
Surprised by canon law, volume 2 : more questions Catholics ask about canon law / Pete Vere and Michael Trueman.
p. cm.
Includes bibliographical references (p.   ) and index.
ISBN 978-0-86716-749-8 (pbk. : alk. paper) 1. Canon law—Miscellanea. 2. Canon law—Popular works. I. Trueman, Michael, 1970- II. Title.
KBU160.V47 2007
262.9—dc22

2007027278

ISBN 978-0-86716-749-8
Copyright ©2007, Pete Vere and Michael Trueman. All rights reserved.

Published by Servant Books, an imprint of
St. Anthony Messenger Press
28 W. Liberty St.
Cincinnati, OH 45202
www.ServantBooks.org

Printed in the United States of America.
Printed on acid-free paper.
07 08 09 10 11 5 4 3 2 1

TABLE OF CONTENTS

FOREWORD

Whether it be from the proverbial "left" or "right," one finds the law of the Church greeted with an almost precognitive sense of suspicion today. In fact, the same law that the left views as a sign of a misogynist patriarchy attempting to keep the Church in the "dark ages" can be viewed as a liberal conspiracy to undermine the sacred Tradition of the "true Church" by those on the right. Yet if the Church is to thrive in our time, there needs to be a healthy sense among the faithful to receive the disciplines of the Church with charity and ready willingness to obey.

The authors' first book, *Surprised by Canon Law*, did a true service to the gospel and the Church in introducing many faithful Catholics to canon law in a positive and understandable manner. In answering 150 common questions about canon law, the authors went a long way toward fostering a healthy disposition toward law among the faithful.

Surprised by Canon Law taught us, among many other things, the reasonable nature of the law. When the faithful see the truth behind the law of the Church, they will begin to see the Church as she is: a mother whose laws have the children's best interests at heart. In fact, one finds an informed Catholic much more apt to view a particular law positively and to obey the law, even when he or she may not fully understand the "why" behind the law.

In *Surprised by Canon Law, Volume 2*, Pete Vere and Michael Trueman give invaluable answers to more questions concerning canon law and an introduction to other expressions of Church law. In this volume we begin to see Church law as an organic whole.

The importance of this work can hardly be overemphasized. It was while establishing the juridical authority of the Church that our Lord said to Saint Peter, "Satan demanded to have [all of] you, that he may sift you like wheat" (Luke 22:31). The enemy of our souls knows well that if he can undermine the juridical authority of the Church through a distorted notion of the law, he can render the Church powerless in the world. Because as the authors state in their first book, it is precisely through the law of the Church that the faith of the Church is communicated throughout the world.

We Catholics are not Gnostics: we know that knowledge is *not* everything. However, there is no doubt, as the prophet Daniel declared, that "the people who know their God shall stand firm and take action" (Daniel 11:32). *Surprised by Canon Law, Volume 2* is a priceless tool that will enable all who read it and take it to heart to "stand firm and take action."

Joyfully in Christ,
Tim Staples
Staff apologist, Catholic Answers

INTRODUCTION

Another Look at Church Law

It became evident shortly after the release of *Surprised by Canon Law* that a sequel would be in order. We were delighted that Catholics and other enquirers found *Surprised by Canon Law* to be of assistance in understanding our faith. Furthermore, we are delighted that you are holding this sequel edition, and we trust that our attending to other aspects of Church law will enhance and deepen your appreciation for this gift of the Church.

When writing *Surprised by Canon Law*, it was a challenge for us to *not* address some canons in the *Code of Canon Law* as well as other aspects of Church law. We needed *Surprised by Canon Law* to be a simple, straightforward introduction to the law as it relates to the questions that people ask. We tried to avoid our specific interests, though Pete was able to indulge one of his passions, the rights of those with developmental disabilities, and I one of mine, the ordering of a diocese.

After we finished writing *Surprised by Canon Law* and were able to take a bird's-eye view of the text, we knew there were gaps in addressing certain parts of the *Code of Canon Law* as well as other expressions of Church law. Perhaps by way of introduction, therefore, our first question could be, "What areas of the *Code of Canon Law* were not covered in the first book?" and our second question could be, "Why are there other expressions of Church law not found in the *Code of Canon Law*, and what are they?"

It should come as no surprise that some aspects of law are not as popular as others. Nonetheless, there are portions of the *Code of Canon Law* not treated in the first book that are extremely important for the good of the Church. They include laws concerning sacred times and places, institutes of consecrated life and societies of apostolic life (that is, religious orders), holy orders (that is, deacons, priests and bishops), the removal and transfer of a pastor, parish mergers, penal law and Church property. Some of these topics can seem a bit ethereal, but we hope in subsequent pages to be faithful to our stated task of making such matters understandable to the layperson. We hope the glossary in the back will help the reader understand some less familiar legal and ecclesial terms.

There is a large body of law that is not found in the *Code of Canon Law*, because a "code" or system of law simply would not be able to handle the sheer volume of content. The most evident example of this is liturgical law, and since the Church has liturgists who deliberate on such matters, we will not broach the topic. We will treat the Directory for the Application of Principles and Norms on Ecumenism; *Pastor Bonus* and the structure of the Vatican offices; *Apostolos Suos* and the structure of national conferences of bishops; *Universi Dominici Gregis* and the election of the pope; *Divinus Perfectionis Magister* and the canonization of saints; and *Sacramentorum Sanctitatis Tutela* and cases of clergy sexual misconduct, particularly in relation to preserving the dignity of the sacraments.

We also broaden our consideration of canon law to include the Code of Canons of the Eastern Churches. This code applies to the Churches of the Byzantine, Alexandrian, Antiochian, Armenian and Chaldean traditions, all of which are in communion with Rome.

Since this book likely will bring to completion a venture to present Church law in a form that is accessible to all Catholics, we must express our esteem and gratitude to a number of people. Our wives, Cheryl and Sonya, have provided tremendous support through these exciting times, and our children have reminded us of the august responsibility of transmitting the faith to another generation. We must thank our esteemed professors of canon law at St. Paul University in Ottawa, Ontario, and our professional colleagues and classmates, whose love for Christ and his Church inspire us on a daily basis.

Michael would like to express his gratitude to Adam Cardinal Maida, archbishop of Detroit; to Monsignors Robert McClory, George Miller and John Zenz and Father Ronald Browne of the archdiocese of Detroit; to Father Paul Baillargeon and Michael Tremblay of the diocese of London; and to Father Robert Nalley and Mary

Dickerson of the diocese of Gaylord.

Pete would like to thank especially Bishop Jean-Louis Plouffe, bishop of Sault Ste. Marie, and Father Bob Bourgon of the diocese of Sault Ste. Marie; Monsignor Patrick Pratico, Joe Fox and Linda Price of the diocese of Scranton; Father Arnaud Devillers, former superior general of the Priestly Fraternity of Saint Peter; and Fathers Joseph Amato and John Dolciamore of the diocese of Venice.

In the early months of discussing the idea of writing *Surprised by Canon Law*, we were clear on one thing: Only the Lord could bring success to such an initiative. We give all praise to him—Father, Son and Holy Spirit—and ask Mary's intercession, that following her example, we will continue to be faithful servants, always keeping before us the good of the Church and the transmission of the gospel. May our efforts be always pleasing to God.

Michael and Pete
January 7, 2007
Feast of Saint Raymond of Peñafort,
Patron of Canon Lawyers

CHAPTER ONE

Sacred Times and Places

1. What are holy days of obligation?

Canon 1247 states that on a holy day of obligation the Church requires Catholics to attend Mass and "abstain from such work or business that would inhibit the worship to be given to God, the joy proper to the Lord's Day, or the due relaxation of mind and body." In addition to each Sunday, there are a number of feasts that the Church in different parts of the world observes as holy days of obligation: the Nativity of our Lord (Christmas), the Epiphany, the Ascension, the Feast of Corpus Christi, the Feast of Mary the Mother of God, the Immaculate Conception, the Assumption of Mary, the Feast of Saint Joseph, the Feast of Saints Peter and Paul and All Saints' Day (canon 1246).

At the outset it is important to acknowledge that the obligation to attend Mass on Sunday has its root in two expressions of law. The first is the third commandment, which mandates that the Sabbath be observed with solemnity. The second, and equally important, is the fact that the Christian Church has come to regard Sunday as the day Christ rose from the dead to restore all things to God. Our faith hinges on the Resurrection, and the faithful have upheld the Sunday observance of it with the greatest esteem to the point of making it law.

Unlike canon law, liturgical law acknowledges that days can be counted from dusk to dusk; therefore, on Saturday evening the so-called "anticipated Mass" can be celebrated, and those who assist at this Mass fulfill their Sunday obligation. It should be noted that the anticipated Mass was meant to accommodate laborers who were required to work on Sunday morning, and it was not meant to replace *routinely* the tradition of celebrating the Lord's Resurrection on Sunday. The anticipated Mass usually may be celebrated at or after 4:00 PM on a Saturday afternoon.

Observance of the holy days of obligation—other than the Sunday obligation—varies from country to country. In many countries, with the approval of the Apostolic See, obligatory observances and formal celebrations of some feasts have been moved to proximate Sundays. The bishops of the United States have approved moving, for pastoral reasons, the observance of the Ascension to the Sunday immediately before Pentecost. Yes, in many dioceses in the United States, Ascension Thursday is on Sunday.

Each country is required to have one holy day of obligation in observance of the Blessed Mother. The Canadian Conference of Bishops decided to observe the Feast of Mary the Mother of God (January 1). In the United States of America, however, the bishops have retained three Marian holy days of obligation: the Immaculate Conception, the Feast of Mary the Mother of God and the Assumption.

Many parishes offer an anticipated or vigil Mass for holy days of obligation. Also, for a good reason, the diocesan bishop or pastor may dispense a number of the faithful from or transfer to another day the obligation of attending Mass or commute the obligation to a pious work.

2. Must we abstain from eating meat on Fridays?

You may be surprised to learn that the 1983 *Code of Canon Law* continues the requirement to abstain from eating meat on Fridays. Canon 1251 states that abstinence from meat or some other food is to be observed on all Fridays, unless a major feast falls on that day. This requirement applies to people between the ages of fourteen and sixty.

The Christian Church did away with a lot of Jewish dietary laws very early in its organization. We read in the New Testament of the discussions among Peter, Paul and others concerning this matter (see Acts 11:1–18; 15:1–35; 1 Corinthians 10:23–33). As the discipline of the Church emerged, we preserved one dietary law: that is, on the day that Christ was crucified, we avoid eating the meat of animals that were typically used for ritual sacrifice. Similar to our commemoration of the Lord's Resurrection on Sunday, we commemorate his crucifixion every Friday. Our *dietary* practice is directly tied to *theological* meaning: Jesus was the final sacrifice to reconcile us to the Father. Thus an ordinary practice reminds us of the spiritual reality that underpins our life.

Canon 1251 envisions that there may be a food other than meat from which it is more appropriate to abstain. This is meant to accommodate sentiments in various parts of the world. In Europe and North America, avoiding consumption of the meat of animals that were typically used for ritual sacrifice carries the meaning for which the law is written.

In some parts of the world, the faithful may substitute, in whole or in part, other forms of penance, charity or piety. For example, the Canadian Conference of Catholic Bishops received permission to allow the faithful to substitute abstinence on all Fridays of the year except Good Friday, and in the United States, the faithful may substitute abstinence on all Fridays except the Fridays of Lent and Good Friday.

We should say a word concerning fasting. Canon 1251 of the 1983 Code requires the faithful between the ages of eighteen and fifty-nine to fast on Ash Wednesday and Good Friday.

3. What is the difference between a church and a chapel?

Canon law lists three basic types of structures in which we worship: the church, the oratory and the private chapel. Such places are set aside exclusively for works of worship, piety and religion.

A building is made a *church* by way of a blessing or dedication ceremony that the diocesan bishop or his delegate conducts. A church is the primary place of worship for a parish community, and each parish is required to have at least one. It is where the faithful gather for divine worship and where the pastor is obliged to offer the sacraments regularly.

Given the fact that, as many saints put it, the highest vocation of men and women is to worship God, the faithful have a right to access churches (canon 1214). This does not mean that churches must be kept open all the time, which would be irresponsible in some parts of the world. Churches usually post scheduled hours of access, and in some cases one can request access for private prayer. The Blessed Sacrament is to be reserved in a church.

An *oratory* is a place of worship that in many ways resembles a church (canon 1223). It is a place where the faithful gather on an irregular or infrequent basis for divine worship, and it is suitable for the reception of all the sacraments. Oratories usually belong to a religious community, but more recently some parish churches are being reduced to oratories when parishes merge.

An oratory is what some people might call a "chapel." The Blessed Sacrament usually is reserved there. Unlike churches, the faithful do not have the same right of access to oratories.

A local ordinary (that is, a diocesan bishop, auxiliary bishop or vicar general) designates a *private chapel* as such (canon 1226). The bishop is one of a few people who have the right to possess a private chapel (canon 1227). Permission of the local bishop is required in order to celebrate Mass and the other sacraments in a private chapel. The Blessed Sacrament may be reserved in a private chapel only with the bishop's permission, and in such cases Mass is to be celebrated regularly there.

Canon law also identifies shrines as sacred places. *Shrine* is an additional designation given to a church or an oratory to acknowledge it as a place of pilgrimage (canon 1230).

4. What names can be used for churches? Can a church name be changed?

Since our churches are sacred places where the faithful gather to worship God, canon law requires that they be solemnly dedicated or simply blessed (canon 1217) and given a title (canon 1218) that corresponds with norms in a liturgical book called *The Rite of Dedication of a Church and an Altar* (Catholic Book, 1989). The title of a church can be

- the name of the Trinity;
- a name for Christ, invoked in the liturgy, or a mystery of his life;
- the name of the Holy Spirit;
- a name for Mary that is used in the liturgy;
- the name of a holy angel or the holy angels;
- the name of a canonized saint, as it appears in the *Roman Martyrology* or its appendix;

- the name of a blessed, provided the Apostolic See has given its permission.

Though the 1983 *Code of Canon Law* does not specify what would warrant blessing or dedication, the tradition has been to reserve dedication to churches that are expected to last a very long time, spanning generations. (The dedication ceremony is far more extensive than that of blessing.) The 1917 *Code of Canon Law* was quite specific as to the requirements of dedication. It stated, "Churches...of wood, iron, or another metal can be blessed but not [dedicated]."[1] A church building that had a lien against it could not be dedicated.

It is expected that once a title is assigned to a church, the church will retain that name. However, circumstances may arise that make it appropriate to change a church's name, such a parish merger (see question 42). If a church was simply blessed and not dedicated, the diocesan bishop can change the title, given a serious reason. In the case of a dedicated church, a title change requires prior permission of the Apostolic See.

5. Can someone be denied a Church funeral?

The short answer is yes, but as we shall see, the Church is very reluctant to refuse funerals. Canon 1184 lists three groups of people for whom a Church funeral can be denied, and their circumstances are quite severe:

1. *Notorious apostates, heretics and schismatics.* As outlined in canon 751, heresy is an obstinate denial or obstinate doubt about an essential truth which must be believed by divine and Catholic faith. Apostasy is the total repudiation of the Christian faith. Schism is the withdrawal of submission to the Pontiff and the College of Bishops. In cases of apostasy and schism, it is unlikely that the persons would have wanted a Catholic funeral.

2. *Those who for anti-Christian motives chose to have their bodies cremated.* Since the very early days of the Church, Christians have been careful to respect the remains of the dead, since we profess a belief in the

resurrection of the body. The Church has been uneasy about crema-tion, but more recently, especially after the release of the 1983 *Code of Canon Law*, cremation is permitted if the motive is not disbelief in the resurrection of the body.

3. *Manifest sinners, where the funeral would give rise to public scandal.* This catchall category requires serious discernment concerning what consti-tutes "manifest" sin. It seems that since the risk is public scandal, *mani-fest* implies that many people would know about the sin. In light of what is at stake, the sin also would have to be grave, or mortal. If, how-ever, a person's sins were both notorious and grave but would not cause public scandal, then the funeral could be provided.

In any and all cases of manifest sin, there is the possibility of con-fession before death, especially with the sacrament of the anointing of the sick. As well, it is our Catholic tradition to pray for the dead, and in many cases celebrating a funeral for a person who struggled with sin is beneficial to the departed one and the living faithful.

It is important to note that if there is doubt concerning whether or not one of the above circumstances applies, the local ordinary (that is, a bishop or vicar general) must be consulted and his judgment followed.

6. What are sacramentals?

We understand that God uses the ordinary aspects of our day to make himself known to us. In the sacraments he uses the ordinary elements of water, oil, vows and prayers to help us understand aspects of him. In similar measure we have sacramentals, which, canon 1166 explains, work in "the fashion of the sacraments."

The Church has come to identify many *sacred* symbols and actions. For instance, we have crosses, the rosary, the Liturgy of the Hours, can-dles, statues, gestures, prayer books, prayer cards, pilgrimages, liturgi-cal garments and so on. The Church blesses these things or actions and sets them aside as sacred. Canon 1171 indicates, "Sacred objects...are to be treated with reverence" and not "made over to secular or inappro-priate use, even though they may belong to private persons."

The Apostolic See determines the various types of sacramentals.

The Apostolic See "makes" things or actions sacramentals through a blessing or a dedication performed by a bishop or a priest permitted by law or delegated by the bishop. Some sacramentals are permanent in nature (for example, a chalice for use at Mass); others are temporary in nature (for example, a prayer of blessing).

Clerics ordinarily administer sacramentals, although laypersons can carry out such tasks if law or delegation so authorizes them. The layperson in these cases must possess appropriate qualities. For example, a catechist may pray the prayer of blessing with/for a catechumen using the Rite of Christian Initiation of Adults.

Sacramentals are primarily for the benefit of Catholics, who understand their significance; however, catechumens and even non-Catholics can receive them (canon 1170). These may benefit, for example, from exorcism, which only a priest with the express permission of the local ordinary (that is, bishops, vicars general and episcopal vicars) can carry out (canon 1172).

A good collection of sacramentals is found in a liturgical book called *Book of Blessings* (Liturgical Press, 1989). A quick review of the index shows that it addresses matters pertaining to the Advent wreath, altar servers, animals and ashes, to name a very few. The introductory notes and rubrics (that is, the instructions in small red text) represent liturgical law and specify by whom and in what way sacramentals are made and administered.

7. Please explain the Liturgy of the Hours. Who is required to pray that way?

The Liturgy of the Hours is a collection of prayer services (liturgies) that are designated for use throughout the day (hours). It has been called the "prayer of the Church," to capture Saint Paul's directive to pray unceasingly (see 1 Thessalonians 5:17) and to sanctify the day with prayer. Canon 1173 explains that the Liturgy of the Hours is a means "wherein [the Church] listens to God speaking to his people and recalls the mystery of salvation." It is a way for the Church to praise him "without ceasing, in song and prayer," and to pray for the salvation of the world.

Clerics typically pray five of these liturgies each day. There is the office of readings, which one may read or recite at any time during the day. Morning prayer is known as *lauds*, evening prayer is called *vespers*, and the prayer before going to bed is known as *compline*. There are three minor hours, of which clerics are obliged to pray only one.

The basic shape of morning and evening prayer involves an invitatory (usually Psalm 95, "inviting" the faithful to come into God's presence, praise him and listen to him), an opening hymn, the recitation (or singing) of psalms, a reading of a verse from Scripture and recitation (or singing) of a canticle or canticles from the New Testament. The hour concludes with intercessory prayer, the Lord's Prayer and a closing prayer. The office of readings includes selections from Scripture and the Church fathers.

As you can imagine, the volume of Scripture, prayer and writings is extensive. The English edition of *The Liturgy of the Hours* appears in four Bible-size volumes (Catholic Book, 2000).

A primary responsibility of clerics (bishops, priests and deacons) is to pray, insofar as possible, five of the hours every day. Though permanent deacons are required to pray the Liturgy of the Hours, they may not be required to observe all five of the hours (canon 276, paragraph 2, 3). For example, in the United States permanent deacons are required to pray only morning and evening prayer.[2]

Religious brothers and sisters who belong to institutes of consecrated life and societies of apostolic life (see chapter 3) are also required to pray the Liturgy of the Hours. And since it is the prayer of the Church, canon 1174, paragraph 2 states: "Others also of Christ's faithful are earnestly invited...to take part in the liturgy of the hours as an action of the Church." Many laypersons use a condensed version of the hours, called simply *Christian Prayer* (Catholic Book, 1999).

CHAPTER TWO

Holy Orders

8. What is the sacrament of holy orders?

No large society can function purely on the goodwill of its members. Just as the Church requires rules and laws to maintain good order, so too does it require people who will take charge in various pastoral situations and provide leadership to the Christian faithful. Thus Christ instituted a sacred priesthood to oversee the spiritual care of those who believe in him.

Canon 1008 defines holy orders as the sacrament by which some members of the Christian faithful are set apart for special ministry among God's people. These men receive a special mark upon their soul, which no human power can remove. Thus the sacrament of holy orders is similar to baptism and confirmation in that it cannot be repeated. Once ordained, the man is a cleric.

Because Christ is the Second Person of the Holy Trinity, the sacrament of holy orders, like all the other sacraments, is of divine institution. Those who receive this sacrament participate in Christ's priesthood over the Christian faithful. This means that the minister is set apart to fulfill, in the name of Christ, the functions of teaching, sanctifying and governing fellow believers. Each minister participates according to one of three grades, which canon 1009, paragraph 1 defines as the episcopate, the presbyterate and the diaconate.

The bishop receives the fullness of holy orders, in that he becomes by his consecration a successor to the apostles. He has the power and authority to administer all seven sacraments. Presbyters (or priests who are not bishops) and deacons receive a lesser share of holy orders. The term *cleric* applies to those who receive any of the three grades of holy orders.

9. How and where should an ordination be celebrated?

The second paragraph of canon 1009 discusses the conferral of holy orders. The minister of the sacrament, who is always a bishop, imposes his hands upon the candidate while praying the consecratory prayer given in the liturgy of ordination.

According to canon 1010, the sacrament of holy orders is to be celebrated during Mass on either a Sunday or a holy day of obligation (see question 1, chapter one, for an explanation of holy days of obligation). Canon 1011, paragraph 1 states that the cathedral church is where an ordination should be celebrated. Nevertheless, both canons allow for the sacrament to be administered on another day and in another location if a pastoral need arises.

For example, permanent deacons are often married men who have settled with their respective families in a local parish. Prior to answering God's call to the diaconate, the candidates generally will have served their local parish in a variety of lay positions of leadership. This home parish is often the one in which they hope to serve as a permanent deacon. Thus many diocesan bishops feel that it is to everyone's pastoral advantage for candidates to the permanent diaconate to be ordained in the parish where they are settled, and canon 1011 admits this exception. Because the bishop's schedule might not permit him to visit the candidate's parish on a Sunday or other holy day of obligation in a timely fashion, canon 1010 allows the bishop to celebrate the ordination on another day.

Nobody is ordained for his own sake; rather one is set apart to serve Christ's faithful. Thus the second paragraph of canon 1011 requires that as many of the Christian faithful as possible be invited to the ordination. Those invited should include the clergy, religious and laity, thus representing all states of life within the Church.

10. Who is the minister of holy orders?

The minister of holy orders is the bishop who imposes his hands and administers the sacrament. Canon 1012 establishes the minister of holy orders as a validly consecrated bishop. While not specifically stated within this canon, it is understood that the requirement of a bishop as minister applies for validity. In other words, a deacon cannot ordain another man to the diaconate. Nor can a presbyter—that is, a priest who is not a bishop—administer this sacrament.

Because of the power that a bishop holds in possessing the fullness of priesthood, a bishop requires a special mandate from the Roman pontiff before he may consecrate another bishop (canon 1013). This is known as a "papal mandate." This requirement is among the most serious in the *Code of Canon Law*. Should a bishop violate canon 1013 and consecrate another bishop without a papal mandate, both he and the bishop whom he consecrates are automatically excommunicated under canon 1082. The excommunication in such cases is reserved to the Holy See—meaning that only the Holy See can lift it.

Canon 1014 states that at least two additional bishops should join the ministering bishop for the consecration of a new bishop. This requirement is for lawfulness only and does not affect the validity of the consecration. The bishop who takes the lead in administering the sacrament is commonly known as the "principal bishop," whereas the bishops assisting him often are referred to as the "co-consecrators."

While the canon prescribes two co-consecrators, it allows the Holy See to grant a dispensation. Such an exception might arise in an area where bishops are few and far between and unable to come together in large numbers without great risk: for example, in a country ravaged by war or a country like France during the French Revolution, where Catholics were severely persecuted. These exceptional situations aside, canon 1014 specifically encourages the presence of many bishops as well as their participation in the celebration of the consecration.

In June 1988 Archbishop Marcel Lefebvre consecrated four bishops after Pope John Paul II forbade him to do so, and there was only one co-consecrator. The four men are considered real bishops: The archbishop was a valid minister of the sacrament, and the presence of two co-consecrators is for lawfulness, not validity. But all four men and the archbishop were excommunicated because of the lack of a papal mandate.

11. Can a bishop ordain anyone a priest or deacon?

In general a candidate to the diaconate or to the priesthood should be ordained by his proper bishop (canon 1015, paragraph 1). The proper bishop is the bishop for whose diocese the cleric is being ordained. Of course, this assumes that the man is being ordained as a secular cleric—that is, for ministry within a particular diocese—and not into an institute of consecrated life like the Benedictines, the Oblates of Mary Immaculate or the Priestly Fraternity of Saint Peter. These latter do not have a proper bishop. (Question 13 has more information on ordination of a member of a religious order.)

Canon 1015, paragraph 2 states that a bishop should ordain his own subjects, but the same canon makes an exception if a just reason impedes the bishop from so doing. For example, a candidate for the priesthood from an impoverished diocese in South America might be in Rome for higher studies. He may be prepared for ordination but lack the financial resources to return to his home diocese prior to the completion of his studies.

Or a diocesan bishop might find himself hospitalized the day before a scheduled ordination. The doctors prohibit the bishop from engaging in any strenuous activity over the next month. Yet the bishop does not wish to cancel the ordination at the last minute, because all the arrangements have been made and a great crowd is expected.

In each of these cases, the proper bishop can grant a dimissorial letter. This is simply a letter of permission from the proper bishop of a candidate to another bishop, asking him to preside over the ordination. Thus the proper bishop of the South American diocese could address a dimissorial letter to a bishop in Rome. The proper bishop who falls sick at the last minute could invite a neighboring diocesan bishop or an auxiliary to preside at the ordination.

Of course, this canon assumes that none of the parties involved belong to an Eastern Church *sui iuris* (see chapter twelve, "The Code of Canons of the Eastern Churches"). A bishop of the Latin Church may not ordain an Eastern Catholic unless he first receives an indult (or privilege) from the Holy See.

12. Who is the proper bishop when it comes to ordaining priests and deacons?

Before we can fully appreciate the term *proper bishop* as understood by canon law, we must again distinguish between a secular cleric and a cleric who belongs to an institute of consecrated life (see chapter 3). All clergy must be incardinated (that is, accepted) into a particular church or institute with another cleric as their head. Secular clergy are incardinated into a diocese, or its equivalent in law, with a bishop as its head; and a priest or deacon who belongs to an institute of consecrated life is incardinated into the institute, with a major superior as its head.

Canon 1016 identifies the proper bishop of a secular cleric. For a candidate to the diaconate, it is the bishop of the diocese where the candidate is domiciled (a canonical expression meaning where the candidate permanently resides) or where he intends to serve as deacon. There are several reasons why a discrepancy might arise between the diocese of domicile and the diocese in which the candidate wishes to serve.

For example, a friend of the authors resided in a diocese that experienced a population explosion while he was studying for the permanent diaconate. About a year before his ordination, the Holy See formed a new diocese out of a portion of the old one. As luck would have it, the man's family home remained in the old diocese, while the parish he served fell into the new diocese. The friend's proper bishop became the bishop of the new diocese, where he intended to carry out his ministry as a deacon, despite the fact that he resided in the old diocese.

The situation is much simpler for a deacon who aspires to the priesthood. If the deacon is a secular cleric, then his proper bishop is the bishop of the diocese where he is already incardinated—that is, the diocese for which he was ordained a deacon. In all cases a bishop must carry out the ordination within his own territorial jurisdiction unless he has the permission of the diocesan bishop in whose jurisdiction he wishes to ordain (canon 1017).

13. Does only a diocesan bishop possess the authority to grant a dimissorial letter?

The answer to this question is no. A diocese might find itself vacant when the bishop resigns or passes away. Or as previously mentioned, a candidate might seek ordination for a religious order rather than a diocese. The major superior of an institute of consecrated life is generally not a diocesan bishop, and many of these institutes do not have a bishop as a member. Yet these institutes need to have bishops ordain their priests and deacons.

Canon 1018, paragraph 1 identifies those who can legally grant dimissorial letters to secular clergy. These individuals are the proper bishop; the apostolic administrator; the diocesan administrator, provided he has the consent of the college of consultors; the pro-vicar and the pro-prefect apostolic, provided these last have the consent of the diocesan council of priests. Each of these aforementioned individuals is equivalent in law to a diocesan bishop or governs in his place when a bishopric is vacant.

For good reason canon 1018, paragraph 2 prohibits the diocesan administrator, the pro-vicar or the pro-prefect apostolic from granting a dimissorial letter to a candidate who has been refused ordination by the diocesan bishop or by the vicar or prefect apostolic. This supports an old canonical principle that whoever is temporarily in charge should not make innovations when a see is vacant.

Canon 1019, paragraph 1 addresses the case of a candidate who belongs to an institute of consecrated life. The major superior of the institute has the right to grant a dimissorial letter if the institute is a clerical religious institute of pontifical right or a clerical society of apostolic life of pontifical right—that is, established by or with the approval of the Apostolic See (see chapter three). For all other institutes of consecrated life, canon 1019, paragraph 2 stipulates that the bishop of the candidate's domicile has the authority to grant the dimissorial letter.

A dimissorial letter should not be granted unless the proper testimonials and other documentation have been gathered (canon 1020). The dimissorial may be sent to any bishop in full communion with the Roman pontiff (canon 1021), and the bishop who receives the dimissorial letter can proceed with the ordination as soon as he establishes the letter's authenticity (canon 1022). Finally, the ecclesiastical authority granting the dimissorial letter may provide limitations or revoke the letter (canon 1023). That authority's successor may do the same.

14. Who can receive ordination to the diaconate or priesthood?

Canon 1024 clearly states that a candidate for the valid reception of holy orders must be male, and he must be baptized validly. Canon 1033 stipulates that he must be confirmed. For lawfulness he must, according to the judgment of his bishop or lawful superior, possess the qualities needed to fulfill the various rights and obligations of holy orders, and he must be free from any irregularity or impediment (canons 1025 and 1040; see question 15). Additionally, the candidate's bishop or lawful superior must find the candidate beneficial to the Church's ministry (canon 1025, paragraph 2).

Because ordination changes a person's state of life, a candidate must be free to choose ordination. Canon 1026 condemns as "absolutely wrong" the coercion of an individual to receive ordination. Canon 1027 states that candidates to the diaconate and to the presbyterate should receive good formation in accordance with canon law. The diocesan bishop or religious superior should ensure that candidates are suitably instructed (canon 1028) and that they possess the necessary personal qualities to exercise the diaconate or priesthood (canon 1029).

A candidate for the transitional diaconate—that is, a diaconal candidate who aspires to become a priest—must complete his twenty-third year before he lawfully can receive ordination to the diaconate (canon 1031, paragraph 1): this would be the day after the candidate's twenty-third birthday. To be ordained a priest lawfully, the candidate must have completed his twenty-fifth year of age, and he must have served at least six months as a transitional deacon.

A candidate for the permanent diaconate—that is, a candidate who wishes to become a deacon but who does not aspire to become a priest eventually—must have completed his twenty-fifth year prior to receiving ordination if he is celibate. A married candidate for the permanent diaconate must have completed his thirty-fifth year (canon 1031, paragraph 2). For lawfulness, but not for validity, the married candidate must have the consent of his wife.[1]

To ensure that a candidate is freely requesting ordination, he must author, sign and submit a petition for reception of holy orders to the competent authority (canons 1034 and 1036). Prior to being ordained a deacon, he must receive and exercise for at least six months the ministries of lector and acolyte (canon 1035). The candidate must spend at least five days on a spiritual retreat (canon 1039).

15. What are canonical impediments to and irregularities of ordination?

A man is not automatically suitable for ordination just because he is baptized and confirmed validly. In fact, there are several reasons such a man might be found unsuitable for ordination. Canon 1040 refers to some of these reasons as *impediments* when they are temporary and can be overcome and *irregularities* when they are permanent.

Canon 1041 lists the following irregularities: insanity or some other psychological infirmity that would prevent a candidate from fulfilling the duties of ministry; apostasy, heresy or schism; attempting marriage when prevented from doing so by sacred orders or a public and perpetual vow, or attempting marriage with a woman who is bound by such a vow; homicide or procuring an abortion; deliberate self-mutilation, mutilation of another person or attempted suicide; and impersonating a priest or bishop in the exercise of holy orders or exercising holy orders while barred from doing so. Any one of these irregularities permanently bars a man from receiving the sacrament of holy orders, unless a dispensation is obtained from the appropriate authority, usually the Holy See.

Canon 1042 lists the following impediments: marriage, unless the candidate is seeking the permanent diaconate; exercising an office normally forbidden to clerics, such as mayor or member of a civil legislature; being recently baptized or received into full communion with the Church.

Each of these impediments can be overcome without resorting to dispensation. For example, the authors know several widowers who sought ordination after their wives passed away, and one of the authors is a friend of a pro-life politician who has considered resigning from elected office to pursue a priestly vocation.

An individual might be irregular for the exercise of orders already received. Canon 1044, paragraph 1 lists several types of irregularities that can prevent a validly ordained bishop, priest or deacon from lawfully acting in the grade of ordination he received. These irregularities correspond to those of canon 1041 with one exception: Any schism, heresy or apostasy must be widely known before it can prevent a cleric from exercising orders. While the diocesan bishop may dispense a man from some irregularities, other irregularities are reserved to the Holy See.

Similarly, a cleric may be impeded from exercising holy orders if he was ordained while under any impediment listed in canon 1042. He also may be impeded if he suffers from a temporary form of insanity or psychological infirmity (canon 1044, paragraph 2).

16. What type of documentation is required before a bishop proceeds with the ordination of a candidate to the diaconate or the priesthood?

Canon law lists several types of documentation required by the bishop before ordaining a candidate. Canon 1050 requires a testimonial that the candidate has completed his seminary studies in accordance with canon law. These studies should give the candidate a firm foundation in philosophy and theology, as well as spiritual and pastoral formation.

When a candidate is seeking the diaconate, he needs to supply a testimonial that he has received baptism and confirmation and has been installed as lector and acolyte. He must submit a testimonial stating that he is seeking ordination freely and that he wishes to devote himself freely to the Church's ministry. If the candidate for the diaconate is married, then a testimonial must confirm the celebration of the marriage and the consent of the candidate's wife to her husband's ordination. When a candidate seeks the priesthood, canon 1050 requires a testimonial that he has already received the transitional diaconate.

One of the testimonials should come from the rector of the seminary or house of formation where the candidate studied (canon 1051). This testimonial should note the candidate's qualifications for pastoral ministry, soundness of doctrine, piety, aptitude for ministry and physical and mental health. The canon also allows the bishop to pursue other means of investigation, depending upon circumstances.

If the bishop is ordaining his own subject, canon 1052 requires him to have the aforementioned documents available to prove the suitability of the candidate. If the bishop is ordaining one who is not his own subject, then it suffices that the dimissorial letter (see question 11) document the testimonials and the suitability of the candidate. If the candidate belongs to an institute of consecrated life, the letter must confirm that the candidate is received definitively into the institute and is subject to the superior granting the dimissorial letter. If the ordaining bishop still harbors specific doubts about a candidate's suitability, he can refuse to follow through with the ordination.

17. Is a record of ordination kept, as with baptism, confirmation and marriage?

Yes. Because ordination is a public act that changes one's status within the Church, the Church finds it prudent to keep a permanent record of the event. Thus canon 1053, paragraph 1 requires the diocese where the ordination takes place to keep a careful record of the event. This record should be contained in a special register in the chancery office. It should list the names of the ordained, the name of the bishop who ordained them and the time and place of the ordination. The documents associated with individual ordinations are to be carefully preserved in the chancery office.

The second paragraph of canon 1053 also requires the ordaining bishop to give each of the newly ordained a document testifying to the authenticity of the ordination. In cases where the priest or deacon required a dimissorial letter, the testimonial must be shown to the ordinary (or proper bishop or religious superior) of the newly ordained. The information should be copied into a special register of the proper diocese.

Finally, canon 1054 requires that the church of baptism of the newly ordained be notified so that the ordination can be noted in the individual's baptismal record. This responsibility falls upon the local ordinary in the cases of secular clergy and on the major superior of clergy ordained for religious orders and other institutes of consecrated life.

CHAPTER THREE

Institutes of Consecrated Life

18. What is consecrated life?

Anyone who grew up Catholic will probably remember being taught by a religious sister at some point. Whether Sister taught at the parochial school, oversaw CCD instruction at the parish or organized the annual youth retreat, you knew that she was somehow different from the laity, yet she was not a priest. Like Father she had dedicated her life to serving the Church, even giving up the right to marry and have a family of her own. However, she could not preside over the Eucharist, administer the other sacraments or preach the homily—all of which require sacred orders.

From among both the clergy and the laity, Christ calls some people to consecrate their lives to him in a special way. Canon 573 teaches that the consecrated life is a stable form of life within the Church in which the candidate professes the evangelical counsels of chastity, poverty and obedience. These counsels are drawn from the life and teaching of our Lord Jesus Christ, and they are among his divine gifts to the Church (canon 575). Through them the consecrated individual totally dedicates himself or herself to God's honor, the Church, the salvation of souls, service to God's kingdom and the perfection of his or her prayer, actions and virtues. It is a function of competent Church authority to regulate or monitor the practice of the evangelical counsels and to approve new institutes in which they are practiced (canon 576).

Because the consecrated life makes an important contribution to the Church's life and holiness, Christ's faithful should promote and foster it (canon 574). Those whom God calls to the consecrated life contribute in a special way to the salvation of souls and the Church's mission in this regard. Thus canon 597 teaches that any Catholic who possesses the necessary desire and qualities required by canon law should, after suitable preparation, be permitted to become part of an institute of consecrated life.

Only the Holy See can authorize new forms of consecrated life (canon 605). Nevertheless, the Holy See relies upon diocesan bishops to discern and foster any new forms of consecrated life.

19. What are institutes of consecrated life?

The Christian faithful must be free to assume the consecrated state. They do so through institutes of consecrated life that the Church has erected in accordance with canon law. The individual binds himself or herself through vows or promises to observe the evangelical counsels as practiced within a particular institute. You have no doubt heard of some of these institutes, like the Benedictines, the Carmelites and the Oblates of Mary Immaculate.

The *Code of Canon Law* has a lot to say about institutes of consecrated life: It devotes canons 573 to 746 to this topic. Canon 588 explains, "In itself, the state of consecrated life is neither clerical nor lay."

Not all institutes of consecrated life are the same: Canon law provides for several distinguishing characteristics among them. The first are the distinctions among a religious institute (often called an "order"), a secular institute and a society of apostolic life. Members of a religious institute live together in community, place their belongings in common and make public vows. Members of a secular institute live in the world, either as laity or as clergy (canons 714 and 715), striving to sanctify the world from within (canon 710). Members of a society of apostolic life work toward a common apostolate but do not take religious vows, and they may own property (canon 731). In recent years the Priestly Fraternity of Saint Peter (FSSP) has arisen as one of the most successful new examples of a society of apostolic life. (See questions 21 and 22 for more about secular institutes and societies of apostolic life.)

Canon 588 distinguishes between a clerical institute and a lay institute. A clerical institute is overseen by clergy and is primarily directed toward the exercise of the sacred priesthood. An order of missionary priests is a good example of a clerical institute. In contrast, those who are not clergy primarily govern a lay institute. For the most part a lay institute's apostolate does not necessitate the exercise of holy orders.

The religious sisters who teach in parochial schools and those who nurse at the local Catholic hospital belong to lay institutes.

Additionally, canon 589 distinguishes between institutes of diocesan right and institutes of pontifical right. If the diocesan bishop establishes the institute, it is of diocesan right; if the Apostolic See establishes the institute, or recognizes it as such, it is of pontifical right.

Another distinction is in the nature of the institute's work. All institutes must carefully balance prayer and apostolic work, yet some will focus more on one than the other. Institutes like the great monastic orders, which cloister themselves from the world and devote the bulk of their time to prayer and contemplation, are considered contemplative (canon 674). On the other hand, if the work of an institute is primarily active—for example, teaching, serving the poor, nursing, establishing parishes in mission territories and so on—then the institute is considered apostolic (canon 675).

20. What is an association of the faithful?

Associations of the faithful are founded to promote a work of piety or corporal charity within the Church (canon 298; see question 54). Members do not necessarily profess the evangelical counsels. Most institutes of consecrated life begin as associations of the faithful, but not all associations will become institutes of consecrated life.

For example, an association of the faithful dedicated to networking young mothers with more experienced mothers within a parish community is not likely to grow into a religious order. On the other hand, an association designed to network young seminarians with priests experienced in pastoral ministry could evolve into a new religious institute or society of apostolic life. One of Canada's fastest growing institutes is the Companions of the Cross, a society originally founded as an association of priests and seminarians seeking to support each other in prayer and parish ministry.

An association of the faithful may be either private or public. A private association of the faithful is not recognized within the Church unless the competent authority, which in most cases is the diocesan bishop, has reviewed its statutes (canon 299). The assets of a private association of the faithful belong to the members. Should the private association disband, the assets revert to the members.

A competent ecclesiastical authority always establishes a public association of the faithful (canon 301, paragraph 3). The Church thus recognizes it. The assets of a public association of the faithful are Church goods, and should the public association disband, its assets would remain within the Church.

An institute of consecrated life will often begin as a private association of the faithful, progress to a public association of the faithful and then, after years of growth and stability, have its statutes approved and become an institute of consecrated life of diocesan right. It may then, after further growth, be approved as an institute of consecrated life of pontifical right.

Of course there are exceptions to this practice of gradual progression to pontifical status. A notable one is the aforementioned Priestly Fraternity of Saint Peter, which was founded by former followers of Archbishop Lefebvre who did not go along with his schismatic consecration of bishops. The archbishop's consecrations took place in June 1988. By the end of that year, the Holy See already had erected the FSSP as a society of apostolic life of pontifical right.

21. What is a secular institute?

Canon 710 defines a secular institute as a type of institute in which the consecrated members live in the secular world. The members seek to grow in holiness as well as sanctify the world around them, by working within the day-to-day bustle of life. Whether a member is clergy or laity prior to entering the secular institute, this does not change upon joining the institute (canon 711).

What changes, however, is that the member binds himself or herself to observe the evangelical counsels of chastity, poverty and obedience as followed by the institute (canon 712). The member then strives to live out these counsels in the world, conforming his or her life to the gospel as an example of Christ in the world. In other words, God calls members of a secular institute to provide the secular world with living examples of the Christian message. Thus secular institutes are in many ways evangelical outgrowths of the Church (canon 713).

The living arrangements of members of a secular institute are much like those of ordinary people. Depending upon how the institute's constitutions are structured, members live alone or in small groups (canon 714). The members come together as required by the law governing their institute. They participate in the spiritual life of their institute by fostering its mission and their relationship as members of the institute (canon 716).

Canon 719 exhorts members of secular institutes to devote themselves to Christ through prayer, the study and contemplation of holy Scripture, annual retreats and other spiritual acts. Members should take part in the Mass daily, when possible, and receive the sacrament of confession regularly. They should also seek spiritual direction.

22. What is a society of apostolic life?

A society of apostolic life is very similar to a religious institute. Members of a society of apostolic life live in common and pursue a common apostolate, usually related to the formation of future priests, to work in the foreign missions or to works of charity. The members do not, however, take religious vows.

Members of such a society often are responsible for providing for their own needs. They usually bind themselves to the evangelical counsels in some manner other than a vow—that is, by reciting a promise, a profession or something similar. The society's constitution should define the manner by which members bind themselves to the institute and undertake the evangelical counsels (canon 731). Additionally, the institute's constitutions should define clearly the society's purpose, charism and apostolate.

A society of apostolic life cannot erect a house or establish a community wherever it pleases. The competent superior first must obtain the written consent of the bishop of the diocese where the society wishes to erect a house or establish a local community. The society also must consult the diocesan bishop before suppressing a house or community (canon 733). Once erected, a house has the right to an oratory, where the members of the society may have Mass celebrated and the Blessed Sacrament reserved (canon 733).

Societies of apostolic life fall under the same canons as religious institutes when it comes to what should be contained in their constitutions. For example, the constitutions of a society must detail the following: how the society is governed (canon 734); how a potential member becomes part of the society and what type of formation he or she receives (canon 735); how the society acquires, possesses, uses and disposes of assets (canon 741) and how individual members do so (canon 741); and how a person can cease membership in the society (canons 742–746).

When the society of apostolic life is clerical, the assumption is that the clerics are incardinated into the society. If this is not the case, the society's constitutions must specify otherwise (canon 736). This brings to light one area where societies of apostolic life differ from religious institutes. Whereas religious institutes have their own requirements in canon law for the formation of clergy, societies of apostolic life generally are bound to follow the requirements for the formation of secular (or diocesan) clergy.

Members of a society must obey their superior when it comes to things that concern the society's internal affairs. On the other hand, members are subject to the diocesan bishop when it comes to ministry external to the society, such as the public celebration of the sacraments, pastoral ministry among the local lay faithful and offices or acts of governance within the local church (canon 738).

For example, a friend of one of the authors is a priest incardinated into a society of apostolic life. The friend also happens to be the judicial vicar for his diocese. In matters that pertain to his society's local community—such as common prayer and community meals—he is subject to his local superior within the society. In matters that pertain to the diocesan tribunal, such as annulment cases, he is subject to the diocesan bishop.

Because conflicts occasionally arise between what constitutes an internal matter for a society and what falls under the jurisdiction of the diocesan bishop as a public matter, there always should be some sort of agreement that clearly defines the relationship between a cleric belonging to an institute and the bishop of the diocese where he ministers.

Finally, because they carry out a common apostolate, members of a society of apostolic life are to reside in houses or communities belonging to their society (canon 740).

23. What does canon law say about the evangelical counsels?

Canon 598 requires each institute to define within its constitutions how the evangelical counsels are to be observed within the institute's day-to-day life, ministry and apostolate. Practice of the counsels will be unique to each institute. For example, poverty is observed much more strictly among certain branches of the Franciscans (who are not allowed to own property) than among members of a typical society of apostolic life. With the former a vehicle may be held in trust by the diocese or some other Church entity for an entire community, whereas in the latter each member might own a car.

Regardless, every member of a consecrated institute must live his or her life according to the evangelical counsels, as understood by his or her institute and approved by the Church. This begins with chastity: Members of an institute are to live chaste lives as a sign of what awaits us in the next life. In heaven our hearts will be undivided in their focus on God, as we experience his abundant blessing (canon 599).

Canon 600 defines the evangelical counsel of poverty. Christ, the source of all the evangelical counsels, exemplified poverty in his incarnation for the sake of our salvation. While walking the earth our Lord eschewed earthly riches for the sake of the heavenly kingdom. Thus a member of an institute of consecrated life pursues the counsel of poverty in imitation of our Lord. Such a member should be moderate in his or her use of earthly riches and limit his or her dependence on material pleasures, based upon the law particular to his or her institute.

Finally, canon 601 provides some guidance in understanding the evangelical counsel of obedience. Consecrated persons should follow this counsel out of love for our Lord. They should model their obedience on Christ, who was "obedient unto death, even death on a cross" (Philippians 2:8).

Obedience requires that one submit one's will to the legitimate ecclesiastical superiors. Of course, the superiors must be acting within the confines of the law. A religious superior could never order a member to hot-wire a neighboring institute's car while the latter are at evening prayer. This would violate the commandment "Thou shalt not steal."

The practice of each counsel allows the consecrated member to model his or her actions upon the life of Christ, for God's kingdom and the common good of the institute's members. Thus canon 602 reminds members of an institute that they form "a special family" within the body of Christ, and their actions toward one another always should be rooted in Christ and be examples to others.

24. What is the charism of an institute of consecrated life?

Each institute of consecrated life is as different as the types of ministry and apostolate within the Church. For example, hospital ministry to the sick and dying is not the same as missionary activity in northern Alaska or contemplative prayer within the cloister of a monastery. Thus canon 577 recognizes that each institute of consecrated life contributes different gifts to the Church, fulfilling different needs among the people of God. Charism is that gift from God to the community that inspires an institute to carry out its special apostolate. It is the means by which God inspires the community to labor in our Lord's vineyard.

There is a real danger that over time an institute might stray from its initial charism and extend itself into various apostolates unrelated to it. A burning passion to serve the poor and uninsured might be the charism behind a health care apostolate, but this might expand into a teaching apostolate for nursing students, which in turn evolves into ministry to university students, leading to a retreat ministry for high school and university students and so on.

To avoid this type of straying from an institute's original purpose, canon 578 reminds those belonging to an institute of consecrated life to remain mindful of their founding charism. The members should mind the institute's founding purpose, spirituality, organization, customs and traditions, nature and anything else that forms part of its spiritual patrimony. Thus an institute can carry out well a specific ministry or apostolate, rather than spread itself too thin and watch all its work suffer as it loses focus.

The ancient monastic orders such as the Benedictines traditionally have centered their communities on the expression *ora et labora,* meaning "work and prayer." Thus theirs is the charism of contemplating God through daily work and prayer in the solitude of the monastery. On the other hand, the Priestly Fraternity of Saint Peter was founded to help reconcile the followers of Archbishop Lefebvre with the Church. These clergy live a more active apostolate, and their charism is a passion for the Church's older liturgical forms and the spiritual welfare of traditionally minded Catholics.

25. What is an institute's apostolate? How does it differ from an institute's charism?

An institute's charism is its special gift to the Church. It is what motivates the community to serve the needs of the Christian faithful. An institute's apostolate, on the other hand, is the means by which the institute lives its charism among the people of God. As canon 673 explains, an institute's apostolate is its members' witness of their consecration to God. An institute may join with or foster lay associations of the faithful in carrying out its apostolate (canon 677).

An institute's apostolate may tend toward active work or contemplative work. Contemplative institutes hold a special place in the Church, even though their fruits are not always visible to the rest of the Church. Members of contemplative institutes—such as the Cistercians and the Trappists—spend an extraordinary amount of time in prayer and silent contemplation. Recognizing the contribution of the contemplative apostolate to the Church, canon 674 forbids members of contemplative institutes from being summoned into active ministry, no matter how urgent the need.

Canon 675 then reminds us that the active apostolate—that is, ministering in parishes, missions, hospitals and so on—is the work of institutes dedicated to the active apostolate. It only makes sense that a Cistercian monk should not be summoned to do the work of a Sister of Our Lady of the Hospitals. A member's active work should proceed from his or her intimate life with Christ, and his or her apostolic action should foster a deeper union with our Lord.

Because apostolic action is carried out in the Church's name and with the Church's blessing, community members must perform it in full communion with the Church. An institute's superiors should consult with the diocesan bishop when planning or carrying out its apostolate. This simple courtesy allows the institute and the diocese to avoid potential problems and maintain good relations. Similarly, in carrying out its apostolate, an institute should foster good relations with the diocesan clergy (canon 680).

A bishop may entrust an apostolate to a particular institute (canon 681). For example, many religious communities oversee parochial schools. To avoid future confusion or controversy, canon law requires the diocesan bishop and the institute's competent superior to negotiate a written agreement clarifying the necessary work to be performed, who will perform this work and any economic considerations that concern it.

If a diocesan bishop wishes to entrust a member of an institute with an ecclesiastical office (that is, parish priest, vicar general, university chaplain), he first must seek and receive the consent of the institute's superior.

26. How does someone go about joining an institute of consecrated life?

An individual interested in the consecrated state should begin by contacting the institute that interests him or her. The individual usually will correspond with the institute for some time and perhaps arrange a visit or two. At some point the major superior of the institute will discern whether or not to admit the interested person to the candidacy program and later to the novitiate (canon 641).

Canon 642 specifies that the superior should take into account the potential candidate's age, health, character and maturity. When necessary the superior can rely upon the assistance of experts to help determine a candidate's suitability. Superiors should admit to the novitiate only those candidates who possess the personal qualities necessary to live the life of the community.

Canon 643 prohibits an institute from admitting the following candidates to the novitiate: one younger than seventeen years of age; one who is married, unless the marriage has been dissolved or declared null; one who is already a member of another institute of consecrated life, unless the provisions of canon law for transfer (canon 684) are followed; one compelled by force, grave fear or malice to join the institute; one admitted under a superior compelled by force, grave fear or malice; and one who previously belonged to another institute but concealed this prior to seeking admission to the new institute.

This canon applies for validity. If any one of the aforementioned circumstances applies to a candidate admitted to an institute's novitiate, then that admission is invalid. An institute can enact other conditions for admittance.

Canon 644 forbids a superior from admitting a cleric to an institute without first consulting the cleric's ordinary (proper bishop). Not only is this basic courtesy, but also it allows the ordinary to share discreetly the candidate's strengths and weaknesses as well as any potential areas of concern. The canon also prohibits a superior from admitting those burdened by debt. This canon is self-explanatory in light of the evangelical counsel of poverty.

Potential novices must provide an institute with a recent baptismal certificate or some other proof of baptism as well as proofs of confirmation and of freedom to enter the institute. This last means that the candidate must furnish proof that he or she is not concealing a marriage, ordination or profession in another institute. If the candidate is a cleric—that is, a priest, deacon or bishop—or someone who has been admitted previously to another institute or seminary, he must provide the testimony of the local ordinary, major superior or rector. This law helps prevent unsuitable candidates from jumping from institute to institute.

The institute's own law can contain other requirements that a candidate must fulfill prior to being admitted as a novice. Canon 645 allows superiors to seek whatever additional information they deem necessary to make a prudent decision, even secretly when appropriate.

27. What is a novitiate?

The novitiate is an exciting time for aspiring religious. Like the seminary for seminarians discerning a possible vocation to the priesthood, the novitiate is where potential religious first immerse themselves in religious life. Novices receive the spiritual, mental, educational and even physical formation necessary for a lifetime of ministry (canon 646). Those charged with this formation will test candidates' vocations and suitability.

Therefore canon 647 requires, for validity, that the novitiate take place in a proper house of formation. Such a house is designed specifically to form novices. The superior may allow novices to receive part of their formation in a suitable house of formation administered by another institute.

For validity the novice must spend at least twelve months living in the institute's novitiate community, although he or she may be assigned to another local community to experience the institute's apostolate. For example, a novice with a teaching order might spend a week or two as a teacher's assistant in one of the parochial schools administered by the institute. Yet canon 648 limits the novitiate to two years, and canon

649 does not permit a novice to be absent from the novitiate house for more than three months. Canon 649 applies for validity, and it holds regardless of whether an absence is continuous or broken up throughout the novitiate. In other words, if a novice spends more than three months away from the novitiate house during the twelve months required for validity, the novitiate is invalid.

Canon 650 specifies that a director is responsible for forming novices, and he or she must have professed permanent vows with the institute (canon 651). The director can have assistants, if needed, to help him or her guide the novices and test their vocations (canon 652).

The director must lead the novices to deepen their cultivation of Christian virtues; their prayer life; their contemplative prayer; their sense of worship through the sacred liturgy; their understanding of living according to the evangelical counsels of poverty, chastity and obedience; their understanding of the character and spirit of the institute; their knowledge and experience of all things associated with the institute; and their love of the Church.

Novices should not be distracted with tasks and studies that do not directly relate to their formation. A novice is free to leave the institute at any time during his or her novitiate; likewise, the institute's competent superior can dismiss a novice at any point during the novitiate (canon 653). Once the novice completes the novitiate, the proper authorities of the institute can invite him or her to make temporary profession. In cases of doubt the institute's major superior can add up to a six-month period of additional discernment to the novitiate.

28. What is religious profession? What is the difference between temporary vows and perpetual vows?

Religious profession is the ceremony in which a member of an institute takes a public vow to observe the evangelical counsels of poverty, chastity and obedience (canon 654). Through this profession of vows, the individual consecrates himself or herself to God and incorporates himself or herself into the institute. The professed member then assumes the rights and obligations associated with the institute. For example, the member can begin wearing the habit of professed members.

Perpetual profession is to be preceded by a period of temporary profession. Canon 655 requires the period of temporary profession to last between three and six years. For validity canon 656 requires that the person making the temporary profession be at least eighteen years of age; have finished the novitiate; have been freely admitted to the profession of temporary vows; have not been coerced into professing the vows through force, grave fear or deceit; and profess to a competent superior (or representative) who freely receives the profession.

When the period of temporary profession comes to an end, and the religious is found suitable, he or she must either petition to profess permanent vows or leave the institute (canon 657). This is to prevent the religious equivalent of "shacking up," whereby an individual enjoys the benefits of life within the religious institute without making a commitment to it.

The member's competent superior can, for a good reason, extend temporary profession, but canon law prohibits the individual from spending more than nine years in temporary profession with the same institute. Additionally, the candidate for perpetual profession must, for validity, be at least twenty-one years of age and have spent at least three years in temporary profession.

29. What are the rights and obligations particular to members of an institute?

The *Code of Canon Law* devotes canons 662 to 672 to the rights and obligations particular to consecrated members of Christ's faithful. As with any other right within the Church, one can expect a corresponding obligation. Therefore the exercise of these rights must be understood within the context of the common good. In other words, no right is so absolute that it could permit a member of an institute to infringe upon the rights of fellow members.

To begin, a consecrated member has the right to have his or her institute's rule of life stated in the institute's constitutions (canon 662).

This means that the institute is obliged to spell out how its members are to conduct their day-to-day affairs in the spirit of Christ.

A consecrated member of an institute is obliged to contemplate God in prayer; participate in the Eucharist daily when possible; read the Bible, pray the divine office and carry out other acts of prayer and piety; honor the Blessed Mother, especially through the rosary; and go on retreat each year (canon 663). Although the Church does not expect its consecrated members to sin frequently, canon 664 requires them to examine their conscience daily and to go to confession frequently.

Canon 665 requires members to live in their own religious house. Absences of a year or longer can be permitted only for health reasons, studies or apostolate work carried out in the name of the institute. For example, during the communist persecution of Eastern Europe, institutes often sent their members to minister to Christ's faithful behind the Iron Curtain. It was not always possible for these members to return home before the year was up.

Canon 666 reminds members of an institute to behave prudently when making use of modern means of communication. Television, radio, music, the Internet and newspapers are all wonderful inventions; however, they can be misused. Religious are to avoid things that could interfere with their consecration to God, especially in the area of chastity.

All institutes of consecrated life are to have a cloister. This is an area that only the members of the institute can access (canon 667). The cloister is more strictly enforced in contemplative institutes, and it is referred to as the "papal cloister" in institutes of nuns devoted entirely to the contemplative life. The superior can allow a nonmember to come into the papal cloister or a contemplative nun to leave the papal cloister only if the matter is extremely grave. For example, the mother superior could allow a doctor to visit a nun who has come down with a serious illness. The canon allows cloister access to the diocesan bishop if good reason presents itself.

Since consecrated members of Christ's faithful live a life of poverty and share all things in common, they are to yield the use and administration of their assets before first profession (canon 668). The goods still belong to the religious, but someone else administers them. In general that someone else can be whoever the religious chooses, such as a parent or a sibling or the congregation itself. Whatever the religious earns or obtains from that point on belongs not to him or her personally but to the institute.

Certain institutes may require a religious to renounce his or her assets fully. To protect an individual from making a hasty decision or being preyed upon, the total renunciation of goods is not to take effect until he or she professes perpetual vows within the institute.

Finally, members of an institute are to wear their religious habit (canon 669); they have the right to material support and sustenance from their institute in carrying out their vocation with the institute (canon 670); and they need the permission of their superior before accepting a position outside of the institute. Thus an Oblate of Mary Immaculate with a canon law degree would require his religious superior's permission before accepting a diocesan bishop's appointment to the position of judicial vicar.

30. How are institutes of consecrated life governed?

Like any other organization made up of human beings, no institute of consecrated life would get too far if every member were simply allowed to do what he or she wished. Someone has to take responsibility for making sure that everything is coordinated within the apostolate. Someone has to ensure that the people of God are ministered to, the institute's assets are properly accounted for and the institute's members receive proper nourishment.

Thus an institute chooses superiors to carry out its governance with help from a council of members. Canon 618 reminds superiors that they are to use the power they receive in a spirit of service, always respecting the human dignity of their subjects as fellow brothers or sisters in Christ. A superior should inspire obedience in his or her subjects, be willing to listen to their concerns and foster in them a spirit of common purpose and love of the Church.

Canon 619 reminds superiors that they are building a community for God's greater glory. Therefore they must ensure that their members come to a deeper knowledge of God through the regular hearing of holy Scripture and participation in liturgical celebrations. Superiors should lead by example when it comes to practicing virtue and observing the institute's lawful practices. Finally, superiors should see that sick members receive necessary care, difficult members are corrected and weak members are strengthened.

Canon law refers to some individuals within an institute as "major superiors." The term applies to a superior who governs the entire institute, a large division within the institute (called a province) or an autonomous house within the institute such as a monastery. The term *major superior* also applies to a vicar—that is, an assistant—of the aforementioned (canon 620).

Canon 622 introduces another important canonical expression, namely, "the supreme Moderator." This superior oversees all of the institute's provinces, houses, members and works.

Of course, a member should have some experience within the institute before taking a position of leadership. Therefore canon 623 requires, for validity, a suitable period of time between perpetual profession and appointment as superior. This period of time varies depending upon the respective institute's law.

Here are some other laws that concern superiors: Their period of office should be for a specific amount of time (canon 624); they must have a council, which is drawn from members of the institute (canon 627); and they are to ensure that enough suitable confessors are available to hear the sacramental confessions of the institute's members (canon 630). To avoid potential conflicts, canon 630 prohibits superiors from hearing the sacramental confession of a subject except at the member's request.

That being said, it will surprise many to discover that a superior—even when he enjoys the support of his council—does not hold supreme power within the institute. This role belongs to the general chapter, which is a special meeting of the institute defined by canon 631. The general chapter tackles the institute's most pressing issues and drafts new laws to govern the institute.

A general chapter is unique to the needs of an institute. Some institutes may hold a general chapter as frequently as every four years, whereas others might wait ten years between general chapters. Smaller institutes may invite all their members to attend, whereas members of larger institutes would choose local delegates. Canon law simply requires that the general chapter be representative of the entire institute and that the institute's law provide for the frequency and makeup of the general chapter.

31. Can a member of a religious institute become a bishop?

The Church normally draws its bishops from its diocesan priests. Occasionally the Holy Father will raise a religious to the episcopate. A different set of canons must come into play, since a religious is subject to his institute's superiors, whereas a bishop is subject to the pope.

To resolve this potential conflict, canon 705 clarifies that a religious who becomes a bishop remains a member of his institute. However, he is released from any obligation arising from his religious state that would conflict with his duties as bishop. Additionally, his vow of obedience is transferred from his religious superiors to the Holy Father.

If a priest in joining a religious institute renounced the right to own private assets or administer goods, when he becomes bishop he gains the right to do so on behalf of his diocese or particular church (canon 706). The new bishop also gains the right to choose where he will reside after retiring as bishop—even if his chosen residence does not belong to his religious community (canon 707).

32. What does canon law say about hermits and consecrated virgins?

Institutes of consecrated life are not the only means by which Catholics can separate themselves from the world and devote themselves totally to Christ. As mentioned in canons 603 and 604, the Church recognizes the vocations of hermit and consecrated virgins.

Hermits and anchorites go back to the early Church. They were initially Christians who withdrew into the desert to pray, do penance and contemplate God in silence and solitude. In fact, many Church historians hold that monasteries began as communities of hermits.

In modern times hermits withdraw from the bustle of everyday life to spend more time in prayer and penance. Canon law recognizes a hermit's consecrated life when the diocesan bishop receives his or her profession of chastity, poverty and obedience and when the hermit agrees to live according to a plan of life that the diocesan bishop establishes and directs.

Consecrated virginity is another form of consecrated life that the Church recognizes. Canon 604 identifies consecrated virgins as those who, having made known their desire to follow Christ in an intimate fashion, are consecrated to God by the diocesan bishop in a special liturgical rite. The canon asserts that the consecrated virgin is wed to Christ in a mystical way and that she now dedicates herself completely to Christ and to the service of the Church. The second paragraph of the canon allows consecrated virgins to associate with one another for the benefit of the Church and each other.

33. What is the difference between a public and a private vow?

The *Code of Canon Law* defines a vow as "a deliberate and free promise made to God, concerning some good which is possible and better" (canon 1191, paragraph 1). The code makes a further distinction between a public and a private vow: "A vow is public if it is received in the name of the Church by a lawful Superior; otherwise, it is private" (canon 1192, paragraph 1).

With no intention of diminishing the significance of private vows, which by their nature are promises to God, it can be said that public vows are much more serious. To be released from a public vow requires the intervention of either the diocesan bishop (in the case of a diocesan religious order) or of the pope (in a pontifical religious order)

Canon 1196 explains that, among others, the local ordinary (a bishop or vicar general) as well as the pastor can release a person from a private vow.

CHAPTER FOUR

Parish Life

34. What is the difference between a parish and a church?

People use the expressions *parish* and *church* interchangeably, but they are very distinct realities. Although the term *church* can have a broad meaning, such as the Church of Christ into which all the baptized are incorporated (canon 96), a church building is a sacred place set aside for divine worship (canon 1214). Comprised of four walls and a roof, a church is blessed or dedicated to be the location where the faithful from a given parish gather to worship God through the celebration of the sacraments and other prayer. It is the place where the Blessed Sacrament is reserved for veneration. It has a fixed address (at the corner of St. Mary and St. Joseph Streets, for example) and requires lawn maintenance and utility payments and so on. You get the picture!

A parish is a bit more difficult to define. It is an entity in canon law that serves the needs of the people within a defined territorial boundary or a group of the faithful of a particular language, ethnicity or some other shared quality (canon 518). A parish must have a pastor (or priest administrator) who cares for the faithful and celebrates the sacraments in the parish church.

A distinction between parish and church is important for many reasons. For example, the creation of a new parish usually precedes the building of a new church. That is, the parish, or the parishioners who likely will help raise the funds for the construction of a new church, are identified before their church building exists. On the other hand, a parish brought about by the merger of several existing parishes may have a number of churches at its disposal. This poses its own set of unique difficulties, because the newly merged parish will have to decide which churches to maintain and use.

35. For how long are priests assigned to a parish?

Prior to the Second Vatican Council, the practice was to appoint pastors without a set term. It was common for pastors to stay in the same parish for most of their years of ministry. Since the council, pastors have remained in assignments for much shorter periods of time, partly due to the fact that pastors want to move. Leadership can be very difficult, and shorter terms of office provide freedom for the pastor to move if his ministry becomes extremely taxing on him (or on the parish) or even ineffective.

The *Code of Canon Law* permits the conference of bishops in a nation to assign a length of time to the term of office for pastors. In the United States and Canada, the term is set at six years. The bishop is not free to assign a shorter or longer term; however, he may observe the universal law, which is to appoint a pastor without any term. If a pastor is coming to the end of his six-year term, the bishop can renew his assignment for another six years, provided this is agreeable to both the pastor and the bishop.

The law emphasizes the fact that when a pastor is assigned to a parish, he should anticipate a good number of years working with those parishioners. Stability affords him the necessary time to learn about the people of the parish and to flesh out a vision for the parish. He can build relationships and call forth gifts. Thus he truly can be what his title signifies: a shepherd who knows his sheep, who walks with them and cares for them. Friendships in the parish also can sustain the pastor's spiritual and personal growth.

We need to make a distinction between priests who are pastors and those who are not. The diocesan bishop may obligate priests appointed to the role of parish administrator or parochial vicar (that is, assistant to the parish priest) to move, as necessary, in response to the needs of the faithful. The bishop also can ask priests to resign their positions.

36. Under what circumstances might a bishop remove a pastor from his role?

Canon 1740 states that when a pastor's ministry becomes harmful or at least ineffective, the bishop can remove him from his role. The focus is on the pastor's ministry *in the parish to which he is assigned*. It does not matter *why* his ministry has become harmful or ineffective; in fact, other people could be at fault. The good of the Church always must be upheld, and the simple fact that a pastor's ministry is harmful or ineffective is enough to warrant removal.

Unlike some Protestant communities, parishioners cannot remove a pastor; it is the sole prerogative of the diocesan bishop to do so. And it is the bishop who decides if the pastor's ministry has become harmful or ineffective.

Canon 1741 expands upon what would constitute harmful or ineffective ministry:

1. *Acting in a way that harms or disturbs ecclesiastical communion.* Recalling Christ's prayer that all may be one (John 17:21), maintaining universal cohesiveness and unity through the college of bishops and the pope is a top priority for Catholics. A pastor who harms or even disturbs this orientation might mislead the faithful. Such action is so severe that it can warrant his removal as pastor.

2. *An illness of mind or body that causes the pastor to be unable to fulfill his duties satisfactorily.* This is an obvious example of what would constitute cause for removal, but it is worth noting that the canon qualifies the fulfillment of duties with the word *satisfactorily.* An ill priest who is able to fulfill his duties satisfactorily continues to enjoy stability in office.

A distinction should be made between removal and resignation. A priest who has completed his seventy-fifth year submits a letter of resignation. If the diocesan bishop accepts the resignation, the priest resigns his office but is not removed.

3. *A loss of reputation among upright and serious-minded parishioners or an aversion to the pastor that is expected to continue.* It is up to the diocesan bishop to determine whether (*a*) reputation has been lost, (*b*) the loss of reputation is held by many parishioners and (*c*) upright and serious-minded people are among those parishioners.

In the case of an aversion to the pastor, those with the aversion must be upright and serious-minded parishioners. The aversion may be measurable by decreases in participation in the sacraments. If an end is in sight regarding the aversion (for example, an aversion due to a priest's cooperation in an election campaign), then removal is not an appropriate action to take.

4. *Grave neglect or violation of duties, which persists after a warning.* This obviously would bring about removal. Note that the diocesan bishop must warn the priest that he has been neglecting or violating his duties.

5. *Persistently bad administration of temporal goods, with grave harm to the Church.* A parish needs to have property and financial resources in order to carry out the ministry of the Church. When these basic tools are seriously compromised by poor administration, the pastor ultimately is to blame. If he cannot overcome these difficulties, he can be removed from office.

37. What is the process used for removal of a pastor?

In order to determine whether or not any of the items outlined in the previous answer have a basis in fact, the diocesan bishop can start a process whereby the pastor has the opportunity to explain his actions and clear up any misunderstandings. It unfortunately happens that mean-spirited people can criticize and wrongfully accuse priests in order to discredit their role in the community. We've all heard it said: There are two sides to every story.

The process for removal can be outlined as follows:

1. *Preliminary inquiry.* The diocesan bishop must look into the accusations and confirm that the pastor's ministry has become harmful or ineffective. If so, he proceeds.

2. *Consultation with other pastors.* The diocesan bishop discusses the matter with two pastors from a group that is established by the diocese's presbyteral council, an advisory group of diocesan priests. If after consulting two pastors he sees reason for removal, he proceeds (canon 1742, paragraph 1).

3. *Request for resignation.* The diocesan bishop must tell the pastor why his ministry has become harmful or ineffective and ask for the pastor's voluntary resignation. The pastor has fifteen days to comply with the diocesan bishop's request (canon 1742, paragraph 1).

4. *Second call for resignation.* If the priest does not reply to the first request for resignation, the bishop must ask again. If the priest does not reply to this second request, the diocesan bishop can issue a decree of removal (canon 1744).

5. *Pastor's response.* The pastor must have opportunity to inspect the documents that the diocesan bishop has collected warranting removal from office. Should he wish to defend himself against removal, the bishop must allow him time to reply in writing to the documents. The diocesan bishop can then decide, following consultation with two parish priests, to remove the priest from office or to vindicate him.

6. *Decree of removal.* If the pastor is to be removed, the diocesan bishop issues a decree of removal, and the pastor must cease all parish ministry, leave the parish house (unless he is too sick to move) and relinquish control of all property belonging to the parish.

7. *Appeal by the pastor.* The pastor can appeal the diocesan bishop's decision to the Congregation for the Clergy in Vatican City. In the meantime the pastor must do all that is outlined in point 6, but the diocesan bishop is not free to appoint a new pastor while the Apostolic See is considering the appeal (canon 1747, paragraph 3).

38. How does the process of transferring pastors differ from that of removal?

In many cases pastors voluntarily will seek a transfer to another parish or accept a transfer proposed by the bishop. Though not mandated in canon law, this dynamic is a regular aspect of the process of assigning diocesan priests.

On occasion, however, a pastor can be forced to transfer to another parish. Canon 1748 states that the reason for forcing a pastor to transfer must involve the good of souls or the advantage of the Church. There may be cases in which a pastor's ministry has not become harmful or ineffective but nevertheless may not be *as effective* as it could be in another setting. In the case of a transfer, the pastor continues to enjoy the office of pastor, transferred from one parish to another parish. He, of course, ceases to be the pastor of the former parish when he assumes care of the new parish.

When a pastor does not propose the transfer, the diocesan bishop must inform him in writing of his intention to transfer him to another parish. This is an attempt to persuade the pastor to agree to the proposal. If he agrees, the transfer becomes voluntary and should unfold without any trouble.

The pastor, however, enjoys the right to oppose the diocesan bishop's initiative, and he can certainly state his objections in writing to the bishop. The bishop then must give the pastor reasons why a transfer is being proposed, and these reasons must be supplied in writing. The bishop must consider the pastor's opposition, in consultation with two pastors as outlined in point 2 of the previous answer. If the bishop still deems it necessary to proceed with the transfer, he must issue a decree to that effect and communicate it to the pastor.

As you can imagine, the choreography required in the transfer process can become somewhat overwhelming due to the requirement to respect the pastor's right to stability in office. For this reason many diocesan bishops prefer to utilize voluntary transfer or the completion of a six-year term as the primary means of moving pastors from parish to parish.

39. How do parishes merge?

Parishes increasingly have to address the question of whether or not to merge. The declining number of priests to serve the faithful, as well as shifting populations, has caused dioceses throughout the world, especially in Europe and North America, to consider restructuring. The recent trend in North America was to "cluster" or "twin" parishes. This model involved maintaining two or more distinct parishes, with their own respective churches and other resources, such as schools, under one pastor.

This has worked in some cases. However, pastors have become taxed with having to oversee the operation of two parishes and all the administrative trappings that come with them. As well, clustering or twinning often postpones addressing the deeper question of declining parish membership and parish financial viability. We must be good stewards of the Church's resources. It is difficult to determine at what point a parish in decline should end its mission and join with another.

The process of parish merger is simple in theory and complicated in practice. Here we have the convenience of addressing the matter in theory, and your authors certainly sympathize with those who have to sort out the merger in practice.

The prerogative of creating, suppressing and altering parishes belongs exclusively to the diocesan bishop (canon 515, paragraph 2). In some instances the diocesan bishop may request that parishes merge, but in other cases the request will come from one of the pastors and his parishioners after a period of discernment. Although there is typically extensive study in moving toward a merger, at a minimum the matter must be discussed with the council of priests, a representative body of priests of the diocese who advise the diocesan bishop.[1]

The diocesan bishop must also consider the wishes of the founders and benefactors of the parish. The founders are those who were instrumental in forming the parish at its inception. Benefactors are those who made major donations to the parish for a particular purpose, not those who contribute to the weekly collection.

There is also a concern for acquired rights. These could be, for example, the rights of a religious community that, by agreement, has provided pastoral care for the parish for many decades.

Once the necessary priestly consultation is complete, the diocesan bishop can bring about the merger by way of a written decree. The decree will identify the fact that the assets and debts of the former parishes are assumed into the newly merged parish. The parish will then operate with one pastor, one parish council, one finance council and so on. The task of bringing together two unique communities will unfold over the course of years, not weeks and months.

40. What happens to parish bank accounts and property in a merger?

Two canons in the *Code of Canon Law* oversee the method of merging parishes. Canon 121 refers to a merger of two or more parishes in their entirety. We can explain its provisions with the example of two hypo-thetical parishes, St. Mary and St. Joseph.

Both of these territorial parishes, within their respective boundaries, were seeing a decline in the number of Catholics. The parishes had been "clustered" for a few years, sharing a pastor and working together on ventures, such as a joint parish fair. The parishes proposed that they be merged, and the bishop agreed.

The territories of the two former parishes became the territory of the new parish. The parish proposed the name Holy Family Parish, which the bishop accepted. The bank accounts of the former parishes were closed, and a new account was created for Holy Family Parish. The new parish assumed both the slight debt of St. Joseph Parish and the slight surplus of St. Mary Parish. The staff members centralized their offices in one building, and there is now one parish council, one finance council, one liturgy commission and one stewardship com-mission.

Both St. Mary Church and St. Joseph Church continue to be used by the parish, with an alternating Mass schedule. It is clear that, within a few years, St. Mary Church will be retained and probably renamed Holy Family Church. St. Joseph Church will be closed and sold, with the proceeds going to Holy Family Parish.

Canon 122 addresses the situation in which a parish is assumed into neighboring parishes. In other words, the parish territory is bro-ken into pieces and divided among neighboring parishes. Take, for instance, St. Christopher Parish, which had been struggling with declining attendance and finances for a long time. A few parishioners argued for its continued existence, but it was clear that there was no future for a parish in that part of the city. The parishes surrounding St. Christopher Parish, however, were doing fairly well. The dioce-san bishop made the difficult decision to force the closure of St. Christopher Parish and divide its territory equally among three neigh-boring parishes.

This was a "tough sell" for the neighboring parishes, since St. Christopher had incurred a $1,500,000 debt in its bid to stay open over the previous ten years. Fair market value on the property would yield only $750,000, leaving a $750,000 shortfall. The debt would be assigned at $250,000 per parish.

It also happened that the religious artifacts of St. Christopher Church would be distributed to the neighboring churches. Former parishioners who were now parishioners of the neighboring parishes were encouraged by the fact that their heritage would live on.

41. Does "parish suppression" simply mean that the church is closed?

As we mentioned in a previous response, parish and church are different entities. It is odd to refer to a closed parish, since a parish is not a building. It is better to say that a parish is suppressed, or perhaps that a parish has ceased to exist. On the other hand, churches can be thought of as closed, since the doors of the church are typically closed and locked when the parish is suppressed.

Recently the Apostolic See has clarified that, though the canon law term *parish suppression* is sometimes used, a parish can never be suppressed really, only merged. This is a good point to consider.

Take, for instance, St. Luke Parish. The parish had been struggling financially for a long time but had managed to pay its bills. When the local manufacturing plant was set to close, the future of the parish looked grim. In subsequent months the number of parishioners at Sunday Mass dwindled to approximately thirty-five, down from a hundred. The collection plummeted, and bills went unpaid. Seemingly overnight the parish was facing a financial disaster.

The parishioners met and asked that the parish be suppressed. The situation forced the diocesan bishop's intervention. In consultation with the pastor, the bishop decided to convene the council of priests to help him consider the situation. The council members agreed that the parish had to cease to function immediately. While the bishop then issued a decree of suppression, he also had to simultaneously address the pastoral vacuum that would result if the former parish territory was not redistributed.

The diocesan bishop, who is responsible for the faithful of his diocese, was obliged to ensure pastoral care for the people left behind. After conferring with the council of priests and neighboring pastors, the diocesan bishop redistributed the former territory of St. Luke Parish to the neighboring parishes.

Personal parishes, which serve an ethnic or other such identifiable group (that is, parishes without boundaries), can be suppressed. Care for a parishioner of such a parish would devolve to the pastor of the parish where the individual lives.

42. What name do we give a new parish?

The *Code of Canon Law* stipulates certain names that are appropriate for naming (or titling) churches (see question 4) but does not give explicit direction for naming parishes. In 1999 the Congregation for Divine Worship and Discipline of the Sacraments provided some clarification: "The name of a parish may commonly be the same name as the title of the parish church." The norms went on to say that if several parishes are merged into one, the titles of the churches from the former parishes are retained, and the newly merged parish, for pastoral reasons, can adopt a name different from the titles of the churches it is inheriting.[2]

If the newly merged parish name is different from the title of the church designated as the main worship site (traditionally called the parish church) the title of this church may be changed for a grave reason if it was simply blessed. If the church in question was solemnly dedicated, the title may be changed only for a grave reason and with the permission of the Apostolic See. Though canon 1218 implies that the diocesan bishop can change the title of a blessed (not dedicated) church, the above-cited 1999 norms seem to favor retaining a church's original title.

Canon law leaves it to the diocesan bishop to erect, suppress or notably alter parishes (canon 515, paragraph 2), so it follows that he enjoys the prerogative of naming them. Nonetheless, a diocesan bishop would typically want to hear from the pastor and parishioners as to what names they prefer.

CHAPTER FIVE

Church Goods

43. Who owns Church property?

The concept of Church ownership has many facets, but from a theological perspective, the Church belongs to Christ. It would be wrong to think that the pope owns everything in the worldwide Church or that a bishop owns everything related to the Church in his diocese. The Church belongs to an enterprise much greater than any corporation or human individual.

Individuals or groups can administer Church goods, such as property; however, the *Code of Canon Law* places strict regulations as to how this administration takes shape.

A distinction needs to be made between property that is owned by a public juridical person and that owned by a private juridical person. The term *juridical person* is a legal way of referring to what we might commonly call a Catholic entity. Both public and private juridical persons must be approved as such by a competent authority, usually a bishop, and upon approval will have constitutions and bylaws that, among other things, regulate who owns and manages the entity's property and goods.

A good example of a public juridical person is a parish. The parish has a direct relationship with the day-to-day life and ministry of the Church and carries out its stated purpose in the name of the Church, and consequently the property and goods it manages cannot belong to a private individual. The assets belonging to a parish are ecclesiastical goods, or Church goods, for which the pastor must submit a financial report each year to a diocesan bishop.

A private juridical person, on the other hand, holds and administers its goods in its own name. Such groups are not normally affiliated with the Church's official ministry per se. They might include groups like St. Mary's Catholic Bikers Association or Youth Servants of John Paul II.

44. Who has the authority to administer and acquire Church goods?

Canon 1273 gives to the pope the right to administer all Church goods. The Holy Father, of course, cannot personally accomplish such an enormous task; rather this canon gives the pope the prerogative to intervene in cases relating to the administration of goods. This should rarely be a problem, since canon 1282 averts such a difficulty: "All persons, whether clerics or laity, who lawfully take part in the administration of ecclesiastical goods, are bound to fulfill their duties in the name of the Church, in accordance with the law." Every administrator of Church goods is required to make an oath in the presence of the diocesan bishop (or his delegate), as well as draw up and maintain an inventory of goods on assuming his or her office.

The diocesan bishop is the administrator of his diocese. He has the responsibility to see to it that Church goods in his diocese are managed appropriately.

However, the bishop does not administer directly all aspects of Catholic life within a diocese. For example, a pastor is the administrator of the parish to which he is assigned; a mother superior is the administrator of her institute.

Calling an administrator the "good householder," canon 1284 outlines his or her responsibilities:

- To make sure that goods do not perish or suffer harm and that they are properly insured
- To make sure that goods are protected through the structures of civil law
- To ensure that canon law, civil law and the intentions of donors are respected in his or her administration and that no harm will come to the Church as a result of nonobservance of civil law
- To collect income and invest and expend it accordingly, respecting the wishes of a founder or other norms
- To make interest payments on loans and to pay off loans in a timely manner

- To invest surplus money, with the consent of the diocesan bishop if required
- To keep accurate records of income and expenditures
- To prepare an annual report regarding his or her administration
- To maintain a secure and comprehensive archive of the association's activities, financial or otherwise, and in certain cases to update diocesan archives with such records

45. Are there checks and balances in the management of Church goods?

Every juridical person, public or private, must have a finance council, which is composed of at least two individuals, neither of whom can be the administrator (canon 1280). The finance council serves as a review board to advise the administrator.

Canon law makes an important distinction between ordinary and extraordinary administration. Ordinary administration involves paying bills, making minor repairs to buildings, paying insurance, paying staff, maintaining a petty cash account and so on. These transactions are usually small in denomination (though some heating and cooling bills can be quite large).

Transactions and other acts of administration that go beyond the day-to-day are referred to as extraordinary. These could include a building project or a major repair, such as getting a new roof. There should be a dollar limit established in the bylaws of the association to define what is ordinary and what is extraordinary.

If an administrator carries out an act of extraordinary administration without the required consent of the financial council, the act would be null, and the juridical person would not be held accountable. The administrator would bear responsibility for his or her action.

An administrator of Church goods must make an account of his or her administration. In a diocese a public juridical person makes an annual account to the diocesan bishop, who in turn reviews the report to determine whether the administrator has fulfilled his or her responsibilities faithfully and to assure that Church goods are not in jeopardy.

46. What is alienation?

Alienation is certainly an odd word, one we don't hear every day. To *alienate* something means to cease associating with it. In canon law the "something" is Church goods, when control of those goods is lost. Canons 1291 through 1296 deal with this process. Canon 1295 explains that the norms on alienation apply to "any transaction whereby the patrimonial condition of the juridical person could be adversely affected." *Patrimonial condition* refers to the stable base of assets through which a group carries out its task or ministry.

As we noted in an answer to a previous question relating to the ownership of Church property (see question 43), goods that belong to a public juridical person are regarded as ecclesiastical goods or Church goods. These goods cannot belong to an individual. Since these Church goods are for the benefit of the Church's mission in the world, administrators cannot give them away or lose control of them at their whim or fancy. In fact, even if all the members of a Catholic association were to agree to give away Church goods, they could not always do so without the permission of a higher authority.

By way of example, let's say that a parish would like to sell its social hall to a private individual for $1,700,000. Since the parish is a public juridical person, the property and goods that it possesses are Church goods. The pastor and parishioners are unanimous in their sentiment that the social hall should be sold, and many feel that the exchange of the building for the money should not involve the bishop. Yet since the Church will lose control of the hall, this is alienation, and, because of the dollar amount, the transaction requires permission of the bishop.

It is worth noting that if the parish were to give or sell the hall to a group of nuns, the hall would move to the control of another public juridical person. In this case it would still be Church goods, so there would be no alienation. It would nevertheless be an act of extraordinary administration, as mentioned in question 45.

Each country has a minimum and maximum dollar amount that relates to alienation. When the amount of the alienation is below the minimum value, the transaction requires only the permission outlined in the appropriate constitution and bylaws of the juridical person. When the amount is above the minimum but below the maximum, the transaction needs to be approved (1) by the people identified in the constitution and bylaws, when the group is not subject to the diocesan bishop, or (2) by the diocesan bishop, when the group is subject to him. When the amount is over the maximum, the Apostolic See's permission is also required.

Currently in the United States, if a diocese has more than five hundred thousand Catholics, the minimum value of Church goods that the diocese can alienate is $1,094,800, and the maximum amount is $10,948,000. For public juridical persons subject to the diocesan bishop, the maximum is $5,475,000. The dollar amounts are adjusted upward from year to year. In the case of the social hall, the value exceeds the minimum for public juridical persons subject to the bishop, so the transaction would require the bishop's permission. He first must acquire the agreement of the diocesan finance council, the college of consultors and any interested parties (canon 1292, paragraph 1).

47. Can I make a donation to the Church with restrictions on its use?

The short answer is yes. It is reasonable for people to place restrictions on their donations, especially if the donation is a large one. Since canon law places significant emphasis on respecting the intentions of donors, restrictions are appropriate and create a sort of contract. In other words, "I will give you this gift if you promise to do the following with it." If, however, restrictions compromise the freedom of the Church to carry out its ministry, then the offer may be respectfully declined.

Each diocese should have criteria for the acceptance of donations, since on occasion restrictions can burden the Church. For example, an agreement was reached whereby, in exchange for a $500,000 gift, the parish was required to observe the Feast of the Holy Angels with a Mass and a supper for the homeless as long as the benefactor was alive. The benefactor lived to a very old age, and a downturn in the economy caused the homeless community to quadruple in size. What began as a good intention burdened the parish finances.

48. Can I name the Church in my will?

In the same measure that any charitable organization can be a beneficiary in a last will and testament, a Catholic diocese, parish or other association can be named. However, rather than place monies into the general fund of a diocese or parish, canon law allows for the establishment of pious foundations. *Pious* simply refers to the fact that the gift will be used to accomplish some aspect of the Church's ministry, and *foundation* means that the assets will create a stable base from which to continue funding that ministry.

Let us use the example of the benefactor who wanted a Mass and a meal for the homeless every year on the Feast of the Holy Angels. The person could, in his or her last will and testament, direct that a pious foundation be created from the assets of his or her estate, whereby the monies would be invested and the interest used to provide meals for the homeless. If it becomes impossible to meet the aims of a foundation, the bishop may reduce such obligations according to conditions spelled out in the canons.

Simply because a person has, in his or her last will and testament, stated the intention to create a pious foundation does not necessarily indicate the Church's acceptance of the gift. Canon 1304 requires the written permission of the ordinary (usually the diocesan bishop) before any juridical person can accept a pious foundation. It is the ordinary's responsibility to see to it that the Catholic entity can fulfill the prescribed purpose of the foundation. This has theological significance, in light of the fact that the bishop oversees the ministry of the Church in his diocese. Since the ordinary must accept a pious foundation, it is a good idea for a person to arrange this well ahead of time.

49. Where does the bishop get money for his personal support and for the operation of the diocese?

A diocesan bishop cannot seize the assets of parishes or other Catholic entities in his diocese and claim them as his own. The bishop has no immediate means of obtaining monies to operate the structure of his diocese without taxing the parishes and other entities. These entities, called public or private juridical persons, are something like companies in civil law. They are entities distinct from the diocese (for example, parishes, Catholic associations, private Catholic schools and so on).

According to canon 1263, the diocesan bishop can impose a tax on public juridical persons "for the needs of the diocese." The tax must be moderate and proportionate to the income of the persons. This has been interpreted, in some places, to mean application of the same tax percentage to all entities, but it could be argued that wealthy parishes should be taxed at a higher rate than those who struggle to pay their bills. In many dioceses a sliding tax scale is used, akin to the taxation system of many civil governments.

The percentage rate of diocesan tax varies from diocese to diocese. For instance, a diocese may be equipped with many offices, such as an office for Catholic schools, an office for youth ministry, an office for family life, an office for pro-life initiatives and so on. A diocese may have a seminary as well, and even if the students bear the tuition and residence costs, there may be other expenses that the diocese must bear. And the more staff and programs there are at the diocesan level, the greater need there is for a higher tax percentage for the parishes and other entities in the diocese. Of course, it should follow that the higher the financial needs, the better the service for the parishes and other entities.

Canon 1263 also permits the diocesan bishop to impose an "extraordinary" tax on people or juridical persons. The extraordinary tax must be driven by a grave necessity. The word *grave* in canon law refers to very serious, rare and unusual circumstances. These could be expenses related to an international conference the diocese is hosting, such as a eucharistic Congress, or the major restoration of a historic church or the construction of a seminary or retreat center. As long as the grave necessity continues, the diocese can continue to impose the extraordinary tax.

The diocesan bishop must consult two groups within the diocese before imposing any tax: the diocesan finance council and the council of priests. He does not require their consent. In other words, if either of these bodies does not recommend the tax or the proposed rate of taxation, the diocesan bishop still can go ahead with his plans.

CHAPTER SIX

Conferences of Bishops

50. What authority do conferences of bishops enjoy?

The conferences of bishops are usually determined by national civil boundaries (canon 448). In other words, there is a conference of bishops for Canada, another for France and so on, as defined by the Apostolic See. There may also be a conference comprised of countries in a region, like the Antilles Episcopal Conference. Any Catholic bishop (Latin or Eastern) who exercises his episcopal mandate from the Holy Father in a diocese or eparchy belongs to the conference of bishops for that country or region.

Some countries have more than one conference of bishops. For example, when considering the states and territories that comprise the United States, three conferences are involved: one for the States, one for Puerto Rico and a third for the Pacific Islands. The United Kingdom has two-and-a-half: Scotland has one, England and Wales have another, and Northern Ireland (part of the United Kingdom) and the Republic of Ireland together have a third.

The conferences of bishops do three things: (1) facilitate collegiality among the bishops, thereby strengthening ecclesiastical communion; (2) adapt certain aspects of universal discipline of the Church to fit circumstances in their part of the world; and (3) provide resources for the dioceses of the country or region and address issues relating to faith and morals at the national or regional level.

In 1998 Pope John Paul II issued a document, entitled *Apostolos Suos*, that comprehensively addressed the nature and purpose of conferences of bishops. *Apostolos Suos* makes it clear that the direct relationship between the local bishop and the pope is preferred by our law and practice, and that one should not regard the conferences of bishops as intermediaries or, worse, as obstructions in relations between local bishops and the pope. In fact, canon 88 states, "The local Ordinary can dispense from diocesan laws and, whenever he judges that it contributes to the spiritual welfare of the faithful, from laws made by...the Bishops' Conference."

Apostolos Suos is careful not to diminish the importance of the conferences of bishops and certainly affirms them, saying that they "constitute a concrete application of the collegial spirit" (14). It states, "The concerted voice of the Bishops of a determined territory, when, in communion with the Roman Pontiff, they jointly proclaim the catholic truth in matters of faith and morals, can reach their people more effectively" (21).

The *Code of Canon Law* extends to a conference of bishops many prerogatives in regard to adapting the universal discipline of the Church to fit the circumstances of Catholics within their particular country or region. A conference of bishops can initiate other disciplinary norms, which, when approved by the Apostolic See bind all the dioceses of that country.

When a conference of bishops wishes to issue doctrinal declarations, it may do so only as an act of all the bishops in the conference, not as an act of a committee. If the bishops unanimously approve of a statement, it may be issued in the name of the conference. If there is no complete agreement, a two-thirds majority vote and subsequent approval by the Apostolic See is required before the statement can be made official (*Apostolos Suos*, 4).

51. What sorts of matters do conferences of bishops treat?

A quick survey of the *Code of Canon Law* will reveal numerous instances in which the conferences of bishops can adapt certain canons to accommodate better the practice of the faith in their particular country or region. Here we cite a few examples of instances in which the Canadian Conference of Catholic Bishops has made adaptations of universal legislation:

- Canon law mandates three years of formation before the ordination of permanent deacons (canon 236); the Canadian bishops allow previous experience and studies to count toward these years.
- Canon 496 allows presbyteral councils to formulate their own statutes; the Canadian bishops specify that the council must meet at least twice per year.

- Canon 522 says that a pastor serves an "indeterminate period of time"; the Canadian bishops specify a renewable six-year term.
- Canon 1083 gives sixteen as the age for marriage for men, fourteen for women; the Canadian bishops have set eighteen as the marriageable age for both sexes.
- Canon 1112 allows laypersons to be ministers of marriage given the consent of the bishops' conference and the Apostolic See; the Canadian bishops allow the local bishop to designate laypersons to preside at the rite of marriage when priests and deacons are not available.
- Canon 1251 specifies that all Fridays be days of abstinence from meat; the Canadian bishops allow Catholics to substitute special acts of charity and piety.

The work of adapting legislation for a particular country or region is only part of the work of a conference of bishops. Other tasks include addressing major events of their country or region that relate to matters of faith and morality. For example, the United States Conference of Catholic Bishops has issued numerous documents that highlight the Church's chief concerns on matters of social policy. A few such documents are:

- *Married Love and the Gift of Life* (November 14, 2006), a treatise on the nature and purpose of marriage
- *Ministry to Persons With Homosexual Inclinations: Guidelines for Pastoral Care* (November 14, 2006), a treatment of the sensitive matter of offering the Church's ministry to those with homosexual inclinations in a loving way, while articulating the nature and purpose of human sexuality
- *Happy Are Those Who Are Called to His Supper: On Preparing to Receive Christ Worthily in the Eucharist* (November 14, 2006), a theological restatement of the beauty of the Eucharist and excursus on how we should prepare ourselves for reception of the Sacrament
- *Charter for the Protection of Children and Young People* (June 2002), a statement on the Church's responsibility and commitment to protect and promote the welfare of children and young people

- *Essential Norms for Diocesan/Eparchial Policies Dealing With Allegations of Sexual Abuse of Minors by Priests, Deacons or Other Church Personnel* (June 2002), a policy on the treatment of those who have been accused of or found to have abused children and young people

52. What is the notion of *recognitio*?

The Latin word *recognitio* means "confirmation." The Apostolic See usually must approve general decrees or doctrinal declarations of a conference of bishops in order for them to have any force in a country or region.

On the surface it may appear that the device of *recognitio* is an attempt by the Apostolic See to impose its will on the bishops of a country or region. This is a severe distortion of the purpose of the *recognitio*. The approval of the Apostolic See has an important theological meaning relating to ecclesial communion and the authority that is contained in the college of bishops.

Pope John Paul II's document *Apostolos Suos* explains that a conference of bishops, though genuinely useful in their particular country or region, cannot act outside the unity that is enjoyed by the College of Bishops—that is, all the bishops worldwide. The College of Bishops acts in unison with the successor of Peter, the pope, who assumes the role of "first among equals": Without him the College of Bishops does not enjoy its authority.

If bishops of a particular conference want to offer doctrinal declarations to the faithful, they must do so with the express consent of the pope. With this consent a declaration becomes an expression of the entire college of bishops. By way of exception, as an expression of confidence when it comes to some matters of faith and morals, a conference of bishops can issue a doctrinal statement in its own name when all the members unanimously vote in favor of the statement.

As previously indicated, the *recognitio* is also required for general decrees. General decrees affect all the member dioceses of the conference and usually relate to matters of discipline within the particular country or region. Although adaptations of universal law are necessary in some cases, an adaptation can be taken too far, to the point of distorting the original intent of the law and, perhaps unknowingly, causing isolation from the rest of the universal Church. As head of the college of bishops, deference is given to the pope to approve certain adaptations of universal discipline.

Clergy and laity alike should welcome the *recognitio* as a necessary device for strengthening and sustaining ecclesiastical communion. This communion is the hallmark quality of the college of bishops, a response to Christ's teaching that we all may be one (John 17:21). The ability to adapt universal legislation allows for diversity, while the practice of *recognitio* safeguards unity.

CHAPTER SEVEN
Offices of the Roman Curia

53. What are the offices in the Vatican?

The pope is both the bishop of Rome and the pastor of the universal Church. The pope cannot attend personally to all aspects of this oversight. In order to assist the Holy Father with his responsibilities to the universal Church, there is a structure in place called the Roman Curia. *Curia* simply means "office."

The offices, which are called *dicasteries*, of the Roman Curia are divided into congregations, commissions, councils and tribunals. These differ in terms of responsibilities and staff. The congregations handle serious day-to-day matters; however, a commission or council may have to also tackle very difficult questions that arise. It is important to understand that these offices exist as clear expressions of the pope's communion with the bishops throughout the world, to assist them in their care for the needs of the faithful and the salvation of souls.

The offices are as follows:

Secretariat of State
Congregation for the Doctrine of the Faith
Congregation for the Oriental Churches
Congregation for Divine Worship and Discipline of the Sacraments
Congregation for the Causes of Saints
Congregation for Bishops
Congregation for the Evangelization of People
Congregation for the Clergy
Congregation for Institutes of Consecrated Life and Societies of
    Apostolic Life
Congregation for Catholic Education
Apostolic Penitentiary
Supreme Tribunal of the Apostolic Signatura
Tribunal of the Roman Rota
Pontifical Council for the Laity
Pontifical Council for Promoting Christian Unity

Pontifical Council for the Family

Pontifical Council for Justice and Peace: Care of Migrants and Itinerant Peoples

Pontifical Council *Cor Unum* (Charitable Works)

Pontifical Council for Pastoral Assistance to Health-Care Workers

Pontifical Council for the Interpretation of Legislative Texts

Pontifical Council for Interreligious Dialogue

Pontifical Council for Social Communications

The Apostolic Camera

The Administration of the Patrimony of the Apostolic See

The Prefecture for the Economic Affairs of the Holy See

The Prefecture of the Papal Household

The Office for the Liturgical Celebrations of the Supreme Pontiff

The Roman Curia operates under the direction of the *Code of Canon Law*, but given its one-of-a-kind status, Pope John Paul II issued complementary law in 1988 to clarify certain aspects of the Roman Curia's constitution and responsibilities. The document is called *Pastor Bonus*, which literally means "Good Shepherd." *Pastor Bonus* gives the various offices the authority to address specific aspects of the Church's life, though many matters are, of course, reserved for the pope's personal attention and decision.

54. What office handles the concerns of laypersons?

Pope Paul VI established the Pontifical Council for the Laity in 1967. In 1976 it became a permanent part of the Roman Curia. It is now listed as the first among the pontifical councils. This is not the only office within the Roman Curia to address the affairs of laypeople, since the laity have concerns relating to a number of the congregations, commissions and councils. Nonetheless, since the Pontifical Council for the Laity was established in name for the laity, we should look more closely at its purpose.

Article 131 of *Pastor Bonus* explains that the purpose of the Pontifical Council for the Laity is to promote and coordinate "the apostolate of the laity and, generally, [be involved] in those matters respecting the

Christian life of laypeople as such." The Council is "to urge and support laypeople to participate in the life and mission of the Church in their own way" (133). The Council is commissioned with fostering the cooperation of lay people "in catechetical instruction, in liturgical and sacramental life as well as in works of mercy, charity, and social development" (133).

One means of urging, supporting and fostering the work of the laity is an international conference. For example, from May 31 to June 2 of 2006, the Pontifical Council for the Laity hosted the Second World Congress of Ecclesial Movements and New Communities.

The most specific task assigned to the Pontifical Council for the Laity is to create international associations of Christ's faithful. Associations of Christ's faithful are officially sanctioned organizations that advance the mission of the Church among the faithful. These associations usually begin at the diocesan level, but from time to time an association needs to be recognized as an international association due to growth within its membership. Recognition by the Apostolic See increases the group's profile, puts it in a more direct relationship with the pope and makes it easier for the group to establish itself in other dioceses. Whenever a group would like international recognition, the Pontifical Council for the Laity must review its statutes (that is, its constitution and bylaws) and issue the appropriate decree.

55. To what Vatican office would I write if I have a complaint about the Church?

A small book could be written to answer this question, so we will consider only a few matters in this answer.

Key to this discussion is the fact that the Church operates on the principle of subsidiarity. That means that before raising concerns with the pope and the Roman Curia, what can be handled at the local level should be. In other words, your pastor or your bishop should be the first to hear about your concerns. With over one billion Catholics in the world and the increased ease and speed of communication, the Roman Curia can become overwhelmed by requests.

Even if you have a matter that requires an answer from the pope or the Roman Curia, it is best to communicate it through your bishop. Your bishop in turn will communicate with the appropriate office of the Vatican. Some of the most common matters and the offices of the Apostolic See to which they are brought are as follows:

- To appeal a declaration of nullity (an annulment): Tribunal of the Roman Rota
- To seek dissolution of a marriage due to nonconsummation: Congregation for Divine Worship and the Discipline of the Sacraments
- To request a new marriage by way of a privilege of the faith: Congregation for the Doctrine of the Faith
- To oppose the sale or demolition of a church: If the concern deals with procedure, the Supreme Tribunal of the Apostolic Signatura; if the concern deals with the decision, the Congregation for the Clergy
- To seek a transfer from an Eastern Catholic Church (see chapter twelve) to the Latin Church: Congregation for the Oriental Churches
- To present a case for sainthood (after preparation by the local bishop): Congregation for the Causes of Saints
- To report liturgical abuse in a diocese: Congregation for Divine Worship and the Discipline of the Sacraments
- To express concern over catechetical programs: Congregation for the Clergy
- To express concern over the treatment of a priest by his bishop: Congregation for the Clergy
- To express concern over the state of Catholic schools in a diocese: Congregation for Catholic Education

CHAPTER EIGHT

The Canonization of Saints

56. Who is eligible to become a saint?

The short answer to the question is that *you* may become a saint. God calls all of us to be saints in the sense that he wants all of us to be holy and to live with him eternally in heaven.

Yet probably few of us will be canonized saints. The Church calls upon the faithful to honor and imitate these models of holiness, not only because of the way they lived their lives on earth but also because of what we know they are doing in heaven, that is, praying for us.

The Church does not make saints; it only observes and acknowledges the fact that from time to time people ask these heroes of faith to intercede for them, and those prayers seem to result in miraculous events that only the Lord could bring about. In naming people saints, the Church is proclaiming that these individuals are with the Lord.

The Church has come to understand and teach that since baptism is necessary for salvation, it obviously would be a criterion for sainthood. It has also been our tradition to refer to the great models of Old Testament faith as saints (Saint Moses), as well as others who may not have been baptized before Christ instructed his disciples to do so (Saint John the Baptist).

57. Whom does the Church recognize as a saint?

The decision as to who is welcomed into the kingdom of heaven belongs to the Lord. Nonetheless, we can say that an exemplary Christian life, characterized by heroic virtues and holiness, is an obvious prerequisite for sainthood. There are also certain extraordinary qualities that the Church has come to identify as good indicators of sainthood.

If a person offered his or her life in defense of the faith, the Church may recognize the person as a martyr. We can be sure that the Lord looks upon this act of fidelity with favor. The Church gives to the martyrs the utmost admiration. The martyrs include Saint Stephen, Saint Peter and Saint Paul.

Another possible sign of sanctity that has occurred on occasion throughout history is the *stigmata*: that is, a person develops the wounds that Christ endured in his Passion. Those who have received these marks witness, even before their death, to the great sacrifice the Lord made for us. Some stigmatics have been canonized, including Saint Catherine of Siena, Saint Francis of Assisi and Saint Pio of Pietrelcina.

Another extraordinary quality of some saints is the gift to advance and teach the Catholic faith. Some holy men and women have stood out for their practice of this gift when it was sorely needed in history. These individuals are referred to as doctors of the Church. They include Saint Teresa of Avila, Saint Thomas Aquinas and Saint Augustine.

Our Catholic list of saints is found in what is called the *Roman Martyrology*, so named because it originally contained only the names of martyrs. In time nonmartyrs were added, since, in a broad sense, all the saints lived and died for the Lord.

The *Roman Martyrology* reads like a daily journal that very briefly identifies the saint or saints to be remembered and celebrated on that particular day. It usually tells where a saint lived or died, sometimes how he or she died and who canonized him or her. Since the Church continues to canonize saints from year to year, the Congregation for the Divine Worship and Discipline of the Sacraments integrates an appendix into the *Roman Martyrology*; the last edition was in 2004. The *Roman Martyrology* currently contains the names of approximately sixty-five hundred men and women—rich and poor, clerical and lay, secular and religious, married and single—from all parts of the world and periods of time.

58. By what process does the Church determine whether or not a person should be declared a saint? How long does this process take?

The process for canonization is not found in the 1983 *Code of Canon Law*. In the past century the Church has updated the process to allow for the increased intervention of experts, in order to increase objectivity and efficiency in considering causes. Pope John Paul II most recently outlined the process in a 1983 document entitled *Divinus Perfectionis Magister*.[1]

The steps in the process of canonization can be summed up in the following way: the death of the individual, presentation of the cause (the person is called a servant of God), declaration of venerability (the person is called venerable), declaration of beatification (the person is declared blessed) and canonization (the person is declared a saint).

Canonization is an infallible proclamation that the individual in question is in heaven with the Lord. Thus the person would have to be dead before the process could start. In fact, five years must pass from the time of death before the canonization process can begin. This time period, formerly much longer, is meant to bring about a sobriety of emotion that promotes objectivity.

The Church recently witnessed a relaxation of this five-year period in the case of Pope John Paul II. In the past it has happened that, due to the acclaim of the people, a person was declared a saint shortly after his or her death. One such individual was Saint Gregory the Great (540–604), a pope and doctor of the Church.

The diocesan bishop, or those who are lawfully equivalent to him (see canon 368), can present a case for canonization. The bishop should seek the assistance of a postulator to coordinate and promote the case. The writings of the person under consideration, who at this point is called "servant of God," must be scrutinized in a report. Witnesses must be interviewed to inquire into the sanctity of the servant of God's life. Reported miracles must be investigated.

Upon completion of the diocesan investigation, the bishop sends a report to the Congregation for the Causes of Saints for further study and possible recommendation to the pope. Theologians and other experts in their respective fields carefully scrutinize the materials. If it is found that the individual's life is characterized by virtue, martyrdom, alleged miracles or agelong public devotion, the Congregation will recommend to the pope that the Church declare the servant of God worthy of the veneration of the faithful. The cause is then officially opened.

A miracle is needed for beatification, and, following beatification, another subsequent miracle is needed for canonization. The diocesan bishop or his delegate carries out an investigation of each alleged miracle, while the postulator continues promoting the cause. With these miracles the Church grows in certainty that the person in question is with the Lord and is a model of holiness and a means through which we can seek intercession.

At any given time the Congregation for the Causes of Saints has numerous cases that are "waiting for a miracle." That is why there is no way to tell how long a process of canonization will take.

59. Who takes charge of a cause for canonization?

There are many people involved in a person's cause for canonization:

Diocesan bishop. As mentioned above, the canonization process usually begins in the home diocese of the person under consideration. The diocesan bishop conducts an initial investigation into the life of the person. He is responsible for investigating alleged miracles that have occurred within the territory of his diocese. It is fitting for him to preside over the investigation, but he may appoint an episcopal delegate to act in his absence.

Episcopal delegate. The episcopal delegate oversees all aspects of the diocesan investigation. He must be present for all sessions investigating the cause, and he presides over a session when the diocesan bishop cannot attend. The episcopal delegate must be a priest.

Postulator. The postulator has an essential role in the canonization process, as he or she represents the cause of the saint. The postulator makes the preliminary judgment of whether or not a situation warrants advancing a case for canonization. In all steps of the canonization process, the postulator will attempt to present evidence that warrants consideration by diocesan bishops and the Congregation for the Causes of Saints. The Congregation must approve the postulator to work in this capacity. At this time there are approximately two hundred individuals in Rome approved for this task.

Sponsor of the cause. The sponsor directly hires the postulator and financially supports the introduction of the servant of God and the various investigations as the case progresses. The sponsor can be an individual, a diocese or a religious order.

Promotor of justice (or of the faith). The promotor of justice must be present for all sessions of the diocesan investigation. He ensures that the interests of the Church are maintained. In consultation with the medical expert, he prepares questions for the witnesses. Through the episcopal delegate he can pose additional questions during witnesses' depositions. He can admit and scrutinize pertinent documents. The promotor of justice must be a priest.

Medical expert for the tribunal. This medical expert must be present for all the sessions. He acts as an advisor to clarify any and all matters that pertain to the medical aspects of the miracles. He can recommend admission of documents to the case, as well as scrutinize those already submitted. He must be a medical doctor.

Medical expert(s) to inspect the person cured. The medical expert or experts who will inspect the patient need to take an oath before assuming their role and must be interviewed by the tribunal. If the patient is still alive, two medical experts must inspect him or her and submit their written reports. If the patient has died, only one medical expert is required to review the medical records and make a report. The medical experts must be medical doctors, preferably specialists in the area of medicine pertinent to the investigation.

Notary. The notary must be present for all the sessions. He or she will make a record of all the diocesan sessions and authenticate each page of the record, including copies for the Congregation for the Causes of Saints.

Copier. The copier produces exact copies of the original acts to be transmitted to the Congregation for the Causes of Saints.

The Congregation for the Causes of Saints. A cardinal heads the congregation. A number of individuals assist him, notably a secretary, an undersecretary, theologian-consultors, a promotor of the faith, medical experts and other experts in their respective fields. The congregation's personnel meet in a special session to discuss the validity of the miracles attributed to the person under consideration. The cardinal heading the congregation and other bishops judge the case.

The pope. The pope decrees the various stages toward canonization. In light of the fact that decisions concerning sainthood affect the entire Church, the prerogative to make such determinations rests with him. Despite the fact that the Congregation does most of the work on the pope's behalf, a very direct relationship is encouraged between the Holy Father and the diocesan bishop on these matters. Recently Pope Benedict XVI encouraged diocesan bishops to be involved actively and directly in the initiation of causes as well as the investigation of miracles.

The pope's act of canonization is regarded as an infallible act. This, of course, assumes diligent work on the part of the Congregation for the Causes of Saints, on whom he relies to scrutinize the material from the diocesan bishop. The pope decides on what day the feast of the saint is to be celebrated as well as what the saint might be patron of, as evident in the miracles that accompanied the canonization process. By the pope's decree the saint is entered into the *Roman Martyrology.*

60. How does a bishop investigate an alleged miracle?

When the postulator of a person's cause for sainthood becomes aware of an alleged miracle, he usually conducts a preliminary inquiry to see if the claim has merit. If it does, the postulator will ask the bishop in whose diocese the miracle occurred to initiate an investigation. The bishop will then constitute a tribunal, consisting of an episcopal delegate, a promotor of justice, a medical expert and a notary. He will also appoint medical experts to inspect the patient and prepare reports that will become part of the acts, or record.

The investigation then unfolds in a very organized fashion, in sessions. The notary carefully documents each session in writing. Each session focuses on a particular task, and the session lasts as long as is necessary to accomplish that task. For instance, perhaps two witnesses are to be interviewed in the third session.

The sessions unfold as follows:

Opening session. The diocesan bishop should preside at the opening session, since it is by his mandate that the investigation will unfold. The tribunal members take their respective oaths of office. The notary formally enters the postulator's letter of petition and other documents into "the acts" (the record) of the case.

Subsequent sessions. The tribunal members hear from witnesses, including those presented by the postulator, those presented by the promotor of justice and the medical expert or experts who have inspected the recipient of the healing. The episcopal delegate asks questions that were prepared by the promotor of justice and recorded by the notary. After each interview the written record of the testimony is shown to the witness to confirm that he or she has nothing further to add. Other necessary documents are also entered into the acts of the case.

Second-to-last session. Once all the witnesses have testified and all the necessary documents have been admitted to the case, the copier must prepare two copies for the Congregation for the Causes of Saints. The tribunal gathers for a reading of the acts, and during this reading the copies are compared to the original for accuracy.

Closing session. The diocesan bishop who ordered the investigation should preside at the closing session. This session involves the presentation of the original acts and two copies for the Congregation for the Causes of Saints. The documents are inspected for accuracy.

The postulator and promotor of justice rest their case. A trustworthy individual is commissioned to carry the copies of the acts to the Congregation for the Causes of Saints and must take an oath to that effect. The acts are then sealed in two boxes, the original for the diocesan archives in one box and the two copies for the Congregation in the other. Each box is wrapped in paper and ribbon. The ribbon is then sealed with a wax seal, embossed with the bishop's coat of arms.

When the documents arrive at the Congregation for the Causes of the Saints, the chancellor of the Congregation confirms that the wax seal is intact. A receipt is issued, and the work of the local diocese is formally completed.

The cardinal prefect of the Congregation for the Causes of Saints officially decrees the start of the investigation within the Congregation. The various Congregation officials scrutinize the acts for their strict adherence to procedure. They determine whether the miracle is in fact authentic and clearly attributed to the intercession of the person under consideration for sainthood. If in the estimation of the cardinal prefect the matter warrants the pope's consideration, he will forward the case to the Holy Father for a decision.

61. What ceremonies surround the various stages of a person's beatification and canonization?

The beatification and canonization ceremonies are set within the context of the celebration of the Eucharist. In a change of practice, Pope Benedict XVI recently directed that the prefect of the Congregation for the Causes of Saints or another prelate should preside over beatification ceremonies, while the canonization celebration will continue to be reserved to the Holy Father. These liturgies usually take place in St. Peter's Basilica or in the piazza outside; however, the liturgy could take place at another fitting location, such as the town in which the saint was born, lived or died. At the time of both the beatification and canonization ceremonies, an official image of the blessed or saint is revealed to the public.

CHAPTER NINE

The Election of a Pope

62. When did the practice of electing a pope begin?

The practice of electing the bishop of Rome has existed for millenia. What has changed through the centuries is who does the electing.

As we know, the first pope was Saint Peter. Those who followed Saint Peter as bishop of Rome were given the principal place of honor among the bishops due to the significance of Saint Peter's mandate and the fact that he lived and died in Rome, the center of the pagan world at the time. The diocese of Rome maintained its importance, despite the decline of the Roman Empire. It continued to be the focal point of leadership in the Church in and around the Mediterranean.

There is divergent opinion as to how Saint Peter's successor was chosen; however, the predominant opinion is that the diocese of Rome followed the practice of many dioceses of the early Church in making the selection by way of election by the clergy and laity of the area. As time went on, the Roman emperor became involved in the selection of the bishop of Rome, and the increasingly important Church in the East, focused around Constantinople, also intervened in the process. Eventually, so as to avoid nefarious influences, the process of electing the successor of Peter was given to the cardinal-bishops from dioceses around Rome—that is, from the so-called *suburbicarian* sees.

Meanwhile, three ranks of cardinals emerged as assistants to the pope in particular capacities: cardinal-bishops, cardinal-priests and cardinal-deacons. It naturally fell to these cardinals to elect another successor of Saint Peter when the diocese became vacant.

Beginning with the original seven cardinal-bishops from the dioceses around Rome, the number of cardinals gradually increased to the current number, which must not exceed 120 of voting age (that is, under the age of eighty). The increase in number was partly due to the nomination of cardinals from outside the vicinity of Rome. In time the cardinals were permitted to retain their responsibilities and come to Rome, when summoned, to advise the pope on various matters.

63. Who comprises the College of Cardinals?

In 1996 Pope John Paul II issued a document entitled *Universi Dominici Gregis*, in which he attended to a number of issues relating to the election of a pope. In the preface the Holy Father wrote:

> I once more affirm that the College of electors of the Supreme Pontiff is composed solely of the Cardinals of the Holy Roman Church. In them one finds expressed in a remarkable synthesis the two aspects which characterize the figure and office of the Roman Pontiff: *Roman*, because identified with the Bishop of the Church in Rome and thus closely linked to the clergy of this City, represented by the Cardinals of the presbyteral and diaconal titles of Rome, and to the Cardinal Bishops of the suburbicarian Sees; *Pontiff of the universal Church*, because called to represent visibly the unseen Pastor who leads his whole flock to the pastures of eternal life. The universality of the Church is clearly expressed in the very composition of the College of Cardinals, whose members come from every continent.[1]

The College of Cardinals is made up of three ranks of members, following the ancient tradition: cardinal-bishops, cardinal-priests and cardinal-deacons. A cardinal's rank does not necessarily reflect his clerical status. A vast majority of cardinals who enjoy the cardinal-priest rank are, in fact, bishops, and despite the fact that thirty or so cardinals are cardinal-deacons, none are actually deacons. An example of a cardinal who is, in fact, a priest is Cardinal Avery Dulles of the United States. Pope John Paul II made this Jesuit priest and professor of religion a cardinal in 2001.

After the pope's death but before the election process has begun, the cardinals must, if possible, assemble in Rome. During this time the cardinals are organized into two bodies: general congregation and particular congregation. The general congregation is made up of all the cardinals, and they attend to matters relating to the funeral rites and the pending election process.

The particular congregation is composed of the Carmelengo of the

Holy Roman Church and three cardinals, elected by the general congregation for three-day terms, one cardinal from each rank. The cardinal dean assumes the most important role among the cardinals and presides over the balloting process.

64. How are the cardinals shielded from the public during an election?

During what is called "the conclave," the meeting in which the cardinals elect the new pope, the cardinals must stay within Vatican City. They spend their time in two places: the Sistine Chapel and the *Domus Sanctae Martha* (the House of Saint Martha).

Domus Sanctae Martha. Even in recent times the cardinals were locked in cramped, makeshift quarters in the papal apartments, even sleeping on cots in the Sistine Chapel. Many of these men were nearly eighty years old, and some were in poor health. In the 1990s the *Domus Sanctae Martha* was opened as a sort of inn within Vatican City to serve two purposes: to be a residence for the cardinals during a conclave and, outside of such an event, to be a residence for cardinals and bishops conducting business at the Vatican.

The *Domus Sanctae Martha* is furnished and provides private rooms, bathrooms and studies. It also contains a common dining area. The cardinals are bussed or walk from the *Domus Sanctae Martha* to the Sistine Chapel at the beginning of each day of the conclave and bussed back at night.

The Daughters of Charity of Saint Vincent de Paul staff the *Domus Sanctae Martha.* This society of apostolic life, founded in the early 1600s in Paris, serves in communities throughout the world. By way of an interesting contrast, the sisters' charism is to serve the poor: They participate in ministry to homeless people, care of elderly persons, education and youth ministry, health care and nursing, care of children, women's promotion, ministry to people with addictions, pastoral care, support of prisoners, service to migrants and work with the disabled.

Cappella Sistina: In the preface of *Universi Dominici Gregis*, Pope John Paul II wrote that the election should "continue to take place in the

Sistine Chapel, where everything is conducive to an awareness of the presence of God, in whose sight each person will one day be judged." The Sistine Chapel, as we know it today, was completed in the sixteenth century, and since that time it has facilitated the papal elections.

During the election process, access to the *Domus Sanctae Martha* and the Sistine Chapel, as well as other locations used for liturgical celebrations, is restricted to authorized personnel. With the assistance of trustworthy technicians, these locations are swept regularly for audiovisual recording or transmission equipment. In fact, no technical instruments may be introduced to aid the cardinals in the election process.

"The Cardinal electors...are not to communicate...with persons outside the area where the election is taking place" by any means of communication (*Universi Dominici Gregis*, 44). They may not read newspapers or periodicals, listen to the radio or watch television during the election. In cases of "proven and urgent necessity," a cardinal, with the permission of the particular congregation of the College of Cardinals, may have contact with those outside the conclave.

Universi Dominici Gregis specifies that a number of priest confessors should be available to the cardinals at all times, as well as two medical doctors and nurses, when requested by the cardinals and approved by the particular congregation. Two priests are nominated to provide meditations for the cardinals during the election process. There are, of course, housekeeping and kitchen staff present. All these people are "forbidden to engage in conversation of any sort" with a cardinal (*Universi Dominici Gregis*, 45). Further, they must take an oath of secrecy before the election begins. Any violation of this oath warrants an automatic excommunication, reserved to the Apostolic See.

65. What happens when the pope dies? Who oversees the Church while there is no pope?

In the presence of a number of individuals, the Carmelengo of the Holy Roman Church has the official task of confirming the pope's death, and the Carmelengo, or Chancellor of the Apostolic Camera, must prepare the death certificate. The pope's residence is sealed, and the Carmelengo must then inform the cardinal vicar of Rome, the cardinal archpriest of the Vatican Basilica and the dean of the College of Cardinals of the pope's death. The dean has the duty of informing the other cardinals, as well as the Holy See's diplomatic corps.

In keeping with an ancient Roman tradition, nine consecutive days are set aside for the funeral rites of a pope. The start of these nine days should be approximately four to six days after the death. The College of Cardinals must wait at least fifteen full days after the pope's death to begin the election process, and they must begin it on or before the twentieth day.

The Church has no universal pastor between the time of the pope's death and when a new one is elected. Of course, the bishops continue to exercise their authority in their respective dioceses throughout the world. The governance of the universal Church is placed in the care of the College of Cardinals "for the dispatch of ordinary business and of matters which cannot be postponed." The College of Cardinals also takes charge of preparations for the funeral rites and for the election (*Universi Dominici Gregis*, 2). The cardinals are forbidden to make any decision that is clearly reserved to the ministry of the pope, and they may not change laws of the Church that were instituted by a pope.

The offices of the Roman Curia may continue to function but can make no major decisions, since the cardinal members of those dicasteries cease to exercise their offices when the pope dies (*Universi Dominici Gregis*, 14). The only heads of the Roman Curia to retain their authority while there is no pope are the Carmelengo of the Holy Roman Church and the prefect (or head) of the Apostolic Penitentiary. These individuals may submit matters to the College of Cardinals that ordinarily would be submitted to the pope.

66. What is the procedure for electing a new pope?

On a morning between the fifteenth and the twentieth day following a pope's death, the cardinals must gather in St. Peter's Basilica for Mass (called the *"Missa pro eligendo Papa"*). In the afternoon of that day, the cardinals gather again for the singing of the *Veni Creator* in the Chapel of St. Paul, after which they solemnly process into the Sistine Chapel for the official start of the conclave.

The cardinal dean, the cardinal who has precedence by rank and seniority, facilitates the process of having each cardinal take an oath of secrecy while touching the Book of the Gospels. The priest designated to provide the meditation for the day, accompanied by the Master of Papal Liturgical Celebrations, remains in the Sistine Chapel until the conclusion of the meditation, after which time they leave. The dean then asks the college if the voting can begin or if clarity is needed concerning the norms. The voting can begin with the support of the majority of electors.

If the voting begins on the afternoon of the first day, only one ballot takes place on that day. On the following and subsequent days, there are to be two ballots in the morning and two ballots in the afternoon, at least until a pope is elected.

Each morning session and each afternoon session begins with a liturgical celebration and prayer. Following that the ballot papers are distributed to the cardinals. The junior cardinal-deacon then draws three names of cardinals to serve as scrutineers, three more to serve as infirmarians (to deliver and collect the ballots of cardinals who may be in the infirmary) and another three to serve as revisers (scrutineers of the scrutineers).

The election ballots must be marked with the words *Eligo in Summum Pontificem* (that is, "I elect as supreme pontiff") and a space for legibly writing a name. Each cardinal independently marks his ballot and folds it in half. In order of rank the cardinals approach the altar, holding their ballots up for all to see. As a scrutineer lifts the plate covering a receptacle, the cardinal-voter recites an oath: "I call as my witness Christ the Lord, who will be my judge, that my vote is given to the one who before God I think should be elected." The cardinal then deposits his ballot into the receptacle. Accommodation is made to allow the infirmarians and any cardinals in the infirmary to vote.

After all the cardinals have cast their ballots, the scrutineers begin their work, sitting in front of the altar in the presence of the college.

The first scrutineer opens each ballot, makes a note of the name and passes it to the second scrutineer. The second scrutineer notes the name and passes it to the third scrutineer, who notes the name and reads it out loud.

With a needle and thread, this third scrutineer threads each ballot through the word *Eligo*. When all the ballots are counted, the ends of the thread are tied, and the ballots are placed in the receptacle. The scrutineers then add up the votes obtained and record this information on a separate piece of paper.

The revisers then check the ballots and the notes the scrutineers have made. If two-thirds of the college did not vote for the same person, another round of balloting is required (except in the case of a first session occurring in the afternoon). The unsuccessful first-round ballots will not be burned before the second round of balloting is completed.

If there is to be a second round of balloting in this first session, it must proceed immediately. The session continues with the same scrutineers, infirmarians and revisers. If the second round does not result in the election of a pope, the cardinals may recess. The ballots of the first and second rounds have to be burned before the cardinals may leave the session. The Cardinal Carmelengo also must create a document recording the results of the session, to be given to the pope after his election.

If a pope is not elected after three days of voting, the college can recess for one day to allow for prayer, informal discussion among the voters and a brief spiritual exhortation by the senior cardinal-deacon. After seven more ballots the college can take another such break. This routine can continue until the thirty-third or thirty-fourth unsuccessful ballot—that is, through the seventeenth voting session.

The cardinals can take a final recess. When the balloting resumes, the cardinals may reduce the list of nominees to two names. The voting continues until a pope is elected by absolute majority (that is, the votes of two-thirds or more of the cardinals).[2]

Cardinals who arrive after the conclave has begun are permitted to enter and join the election process at whatever point it may be. Even those who may not be able to attend a particular session of voting due to health reasons may return to a subsequent session. In fact, for a grave reason a cardinal can leave Vatican City and return later to resume voting.

Once someone is elected, the junior cardinal-deacon summons the Secretary of the College of Cardinals and the Master of Papal Liturgical Celebrations to the Sistine Chapel. The cardinal dean then asks the candidate, "Do you accept your canonical election as supreme pontiff?" If the candidate accepts the election, the dean asks, "By what name do you wish to be called?" The Master of Ceremonies makes a record of the name the new pope declares.

Each cardinal-elector in the Sistine Chapel then greets the pope in a prescribed manner, as a sign of respect and pledge of obedience. If the new pope is not already a bishop, he must be ordained as such immediately. He then is led to the balcony of St. Peter's Basilica, and the senior cardinal-deacon announces to the people, *"Habemus papam"* ("We have a pope"), and says his name. The pope then imparts his apostolic blessing.

67. What could invalidate a papal election?

There are three things that could cause a papal election to be invalid.

1. It could happen that during an ecumenical council like Vatican II, someone might argue that, since the college of bishops is assembled, the bishops should carry out the election. Yet election by a group other than the College of Cardinals is absolutely prohibited (*Universi Dominici Gregis*, 34).
2. If someone were to be declared pope with less than two-thirds of the votes, the election would be invalid (see *Universi Dominici Gregis*, 62 and the *Motu Proprio* of June 11, 2007). It is difficult to conceive how this could happen. In *Universi Dominici Gregis* Pope John Paul II did away with the practice of acclaiming a pope without voting, as well as the practice of using a compromised means of selection. The College of Cardinals must vote, in writing, through a canonically valid process.
3. Since the College of Cardinals does not have the authority to

change laws created by the popes, it must adhere to the process in *Universi Dominici Gregis* and the *Motu Proprio* of June 11, 2007. The process is scrutinized as it unfolds by the College of Cardinals.

CHAPTER TEN

Penal Law

68. What is penal law?

The Church possesses an internal legal system to maintain good order and appropriate standards of conduct among her believers. However, individual Catholics sometimes can act in a way that is contrary to the well-being of the Church, of fellow believers or of the Catholic faith itself. As in any society, rules are sometimes broken. When this happens the Church has both a right and an obligation to address the situation. Penal law helps the Church to restore order when the rules have been broken (canon 1311).

Penal law outlines when an offender should be punished, the severity with which he or she should be punished and the purpose of the punishment. For example, some penal remedies are medicinal. Their purpose is to help the offender repent of actions judged harmful to the Church, the individual and fellow Catholics.

Medicinal penalties are also called "censures." There are three types of censure: excommunication, interdict and suspension. When an individual under censure repents of the action that led to its being imposed, he or she has the right to have the censure removed or declared. Thus censures are medicine for the soul, designed to break the obstinacy of an offender and bring about his or her repentance (canon 1312, paragraph 1).

Other penalties are called "expiatory" penalties. The Church uses these types of penalties to help bring about restitution after the transgression of a law (canon 1312, paragraph 2).

A penal remedy can be an action or some type of prohibition. Depending upon the circumstances, it can be public or private. It might be for a specific period of time or until a specific action is completed or a situation is corrected, but it can be permanent. Expiatory penalties are as varied as the transgressions that give rise to them.

When canon law automatically imposes a penalty for a transgression —for instance, canon law mandates the excommunication of those who procure an abortion—the law refers to the penalty as *latae sententiae*. Many canon lawyers—including the authors—use the expression *latae sententiae* interchangeably with the word *automatic*. Thus a *latae sententiae* excommunication is the same as an automatic excommunication.

On the other hand, when a superior or a canonical tribunal imposes a penalty, that penalty is referred to as *ferendae sententiae* (imposed). For example, tribunals in recent years have removed the faculties of priests who sexually molested minors. The removal of faculties is a *ferendae sententiae* penalty.

Finally, the main purpose of penal law is to prevent offenses by providing a deterrent within canon law. This means that the Church would rather prevent offenses from happening in the first place than be forced to punish an offender. For this reason penal law is also interpreted in a restrictive manner—that is, in a manner that applies to as few situations as possible as long as there is no harm to the Church or the rights and well-being of others (canon 18).

69. Who decides when penal law needs to be enforced and what penalty should be imposed?

As previously mentioned, potential penalties are quite diverse. This is in keeping with a general canonical principle that the punishment should be proportional to the offense. Nevertheless, canon law tries to maintain some uniformity and provide some basic guidance so as not to appear arbitrary.

To begin, canon 1313 requires that the law more favorable to the offender should be applied whenever the law changes after an offense has been committed. Therefore, if stealing from the collection plate was to suddenly become an excommunicable offense, a thief who stole while the old law was in effect could not be penalized under the harsher new law.

In the same way, when the new law is more favorable to the offender, the new law is applied. Suppose a particular action ceased to be an excommunicable offense. One who offended while the old law was still in place, but wasn't judged until the new came into effect, could not be excommunicated, even though the crime was an excommunicable offense at the time he or she committed it.

Similarly, a penalty immediately lapses when a new law removes that penalty. So if an individual was excommunicated under an old law, and a new law stated that the offense was no longer an excommunicable one, the excommunication would disappear the moment the new law came into effect.

Canon 1314 distinguishes between *ferendae sententiae* penalties, which do not bind the offender until they have been imposed or declared, and *latae sententiae* (automatic) penalties, which bind immediately. Thus a Catholic who intentionally punched the pope would incur an excommunication the moment his fist touched the pope's nose. This assumes, of course, that His Holiness wasn't simply enjoying a friendly boxing match in his spare time!

Canon 1315 states that whoever possesses legislative power within the Church can legislate penal laws. In general this would be the Roman pontiff and the diocesan bishop. The legislator must remain within his jurisdiction: In other words, a bishop can legislate for his diocese but not for a neighboring one.

A bishop can determine a specific penalty for the infraction of a law, or he can leave the penalty to the later discretion of an ecclesiastical judge. Additionally, when necessary, a lower legislator can augment the penalties prescribed by a higher legislature. Thus in countries where theft of sacred objects is a common problem, the local bishops could legislate additional penalties for those caught stealing from the Church.

Nevertheless, canon 1316 reminds diocesan bishops that they should try to keep their penalties uniform with those of other dioceses within geographical proximity. And canon 1317 reminds legislators that penalties should be established only when they are truly necessary to maintain order within the Church. The canon prohibits lower legislators from establishing particular laws that can lead to dismissal from the clerical state. This means that a diocesan bishop or religious institute must follow the universal law when removing a priest or deacon from the clerical state.

Canon 1318 prohibits a legislator from threatening to impose the Church's more serious penalties when a lesser penalty would suffice. The canon reminds those with the power to impose penalties that censures—in particular, excommunication—should be used in moderation and only for the most serious offenses.

Finally, canon 1320 allows the local ordinary to impose penalties, when warranted, upon members of religious communities in those things that come under the local ordinary's jurisdiction. Thus if a priest belonging to a religious community has a history of preaching questionable doctrine from the pulpit, the bishop could prohibit him from teaching or preaching in the diocese. The same is not true, however, if Father's lectures and homilies are merely boring.

70. Does canon law allow for leniency in punishing those who transgress the law?

Canons 1321 to 1324 establish instances when liability for an offense can be diminished or excused. Of course, the law recognizes that some offenses warrant more severe punishment than others: it would not be fair to mete out the same punishment to the petty thief as to the mass murderer. Likewise, canon law recognizes that circumstances sometimes dictate that individuals not be punished as severely as others who commit the same infraction.

For example, two women procure an abortion. One is an established married professional with independent financial means. She thinks the baby might interfere with a future job promotion or add a few pounds to her hips. The other woman is a scared fourteen-year-old rape victim whose parents have told her, "Either 'it' goes or you go." All other variables being equal, should canon law punish these two women equally? Of course not. While the objective gravity of the offense is the same— the unjust taking of human life—the circumstances and motivations are different.

This is why the *Code of Canon Law* establishes when certain penalties should apply and when they should not. Canon 1321 establishes that a person can be punished for violating the law only if he or she acted out of malice or culpability. Therefore the individual must intend to do something wrong—or know that his or her actions are wrong—to be guilty of an offense. The same canon presumes imputability when the law is broken, which means that the individual must prove that he or she did not know that the actions were wrong.

Canon 1322 treats those who normally lack the use of reason, such as the mentally insane, as incapable of breaking the law. This is the case even when an individual appears sane while carrying out the act. In short, the Church presumes that such folks are not capable of forming the intention of acting out of malice or culpability.

Canon 1323 lists several circumstances in which one is not liable to a penalty when acting contrary to the law: being under sixteen years of age; being ignorant of violating the law through no fault of one's own; being physically forced to carry out the action in question; acting under grave fear of something more terrible happening, provided that the action is not intrinsically evil or harmful to souls; acting in self-defense or in defense of someone else against an unjust assailant, provided that one only uses the force deemed necessary; lacking the use of reason; or through no fault of one's own, mistaking a situation for one involving a grave necessity or the need for defense against an unjust aggressor.

Similarly, the first paragraph of canon 1324 lists several circumstances in which a penalty must be diminished, or a lesser penance substituted. In other words, the law gives the offender some leeway without completely letting him or her off the hook. This applies to individuals who only had imperfect use of reason; lacked the use of reason because of drunkenness or other culpable actions that reduced their mental state; acted in a moment of passion without having had the time to think through their actions carefully; were sixteen or seventeen years old at the time of the offense; acted out of grave fear; acted out of self-defense but went beyond what was reasonably necessary to stop the aggressor; acted in response to someone who was being seriously and unnecessarily provocative; negligently mistook a situation for one involving a grave necessity or the need for defense against an unjust aggressor; through no fault of their own were ignorant of a penalty attached to the law; acted with only partial imputability in a very serious matter.

Finally, canon 1324, paragraph 2 also allows an ecclesiastical judge to reduce the penalty if, while investigating the infraction, he comes across circumstances that would make the crime less serious.

71. Are there other circumstances that can affect a penalty?

Canons 1325 to 1330 establish circumstances that can affect the imposition of canonical penalties. Canon 1325 states that ignorance does not diminish or excuse when it is "crass or supine"—that is, willfully induced. Nor can drunkenness and other acts that alter one's mental state, when they are deliberately induced to commit a crime. In short, there is a difference between a person who murders because he is drunk and has lost control of his common sense and a person who deliberately inebriates himself because he wishes to carry out a murder and knows he cannot do so without alcohol to "steady his nerves."

Canon 1326 outlines three circumstances in which an ecclesiastical judge may impose a more serious penalty than that provided for in the individual canons:

1. An offender ignores his punishment and continues to offend.
2. An individual in a position of authority abuses his or her position to commit a crime. A recent example of such is the clerical sexual misconduct crisis, in which several priests abused their priesthood in molesting minors sexually.
3. An individual foresaw the offense but neglected to take any reasonable precautions against committing it. This is a situation of gross negligence.

Canon 1328 specifies that an individual cannot be punished for an offense if he or she does not complete the act, unless the law provides otherwise. For example, the authors have encountered many women in the pro-life movement who at one time considered an abortion. Some even went so far as to schedule the abortion and show up at the appointed time, then changed their minds and walked out just before the abortion began. In these cases the women did not incur the automatic excommunication for abortion because—as one can witness from the babies accompanying them to these rallies—they never followed through with their abortions.

Finally, canon 1329 specifies that accomplices are bound to the same or lesser penalties for an offense. This includes *latae sententiae* penalties when the crime could not be accomplished without their help. Consider the case in which a Catholic schoolteacher drove a pregnant student across state lines to an abortion clinic. While the student avoids the *latae sententiae* excommunication by virtue of being a minor, the teacher automatically incurs the penalty as an accomplice. This is because the teacher made the abortion possible: It would not have happened without the teacher's help.

72. What is excommunication?

Every Catholic has heard the word *excommunication* at some time or other. Even most non-Catholics in North America know that excommunication is something terrible, the highest penalty the Church can inflict upon a Catholic. Yet the authors have also encountered in their ministry several misunderstandings about excommunications.

To begin, excommunication is a censure and thus a medicinal penalty. The Church imposes a censure not only to punish an individual for his or her infraction of the law, but even more to persuade an individual to repent of his or her actions and return to full communion with the Church. Once a person truly repents of the infraction, he or she has the right to have the censure lifted and substituted for an expiatory penalty or a penance when the Church deems such necessary.

A recent example of this involves the Apostolic Administration of St. John Marie Vianney in Campos, Brazil. This group of priests was excommunicated for supporting Archbishop Lefebvre's 1988 schismatic episcopal consecrations. When the priests repented of their schismatic actions, Rome lifted the excommunications and reconciled the priests to the Church. Thus the excommunications accomplished their intended purpose as medicinal penalties: forcing the priests to consider carefully their canonical situation and the harm they had done to the Church.

Canon 1331 prohibits an excommunicated person from sharing in any ministerial function in the liturgy—including the celebration of Mass; celebrating sacraments and sacramentals and receiving the sacraments; and exercising any ecclesiastical office, ministry, function or act of governance within the Church.

Not all excommunications are publicly known. For example, consider the case of a priest who had desecrated the Blessed Sacrament in the privacy of his rectory. The priest automatically incurred an excommunication, but it took years before anyone knew about it because he had carried out the action in secret. Until the offense came to the bishop's attention several years later, only the priest knew of his excommunication.

An excommunication may be made public in one of two ways. If the excommunication is *ferendae sententiae*, an ecclesiastical judge imposes or declares it. *Latae sententiae* (automatic) excommunications, on the other hand, are made public when a competent Church superior declares them. For example, the Holy See publicly declared Archbishop Lefebvre excommunicated within days of his consecration of bishops without a papal mandate.

If a competent ecclesiastical authority imposes or declares the excommunication, then the offender is to be removed from all liturgical functions unless a grave cause precludes it. He invalidly exercises any governing authority he previously possessed within the Church; cannot benefit from any privileges previously received within the Church; forfeits his ecclesiastical office, position and pension; and cannot assume any other position or function within the Church.

73. What about interdict and suspension? How do these censures differ from excommunication?

Interdict and suspension are lesser censures. For this reason they often precede excommunication. They are also medicinal penalties in that their purpose is to encourage the offender to repent.

Canon 1332 outlines the censure of interdict. Those who labor under this penalty are prohibited from exercising any ministerial role in the celebration of the Eucharist and other acts of public worship. They may not receive the sacraments or celebrate the sacramentals. Moreover, if the interdict has been imposed or declared, the offender is to be removed from any ministerial role in the celebration of public liturgy. An interdict, like excommunication, can be imposed upon laity, religious and clergy.

In contrast, a suspension can be imposed only upon clergy. This censure can suspend all of a cleric's rights or powers within the Church or only some of them. Thus a suspension can be particular to the cleric based upon his offense. For example, a priest who swears in public might be suspended from celebrating the sacraments but not from administering the temporal goods of his parish in the solitude of his office.

Canon 1333 can prevent a suspended priest from exercising the power of orders (celebrating the sacraments), exercising the power of governance (granting dispensations or judging cases for the diocesan tribunal) and exercising the rights or functions attached to an office. If the suspension is publicly imposed or declared, the suspended cleric can no longer exercise validly his power of governance within the Church.

A suspension does not affect an ecclesiastical office or power of governance over which the superior establishing the censure has no jurisdiction. It does not affect the suspended cleric's right of residence or, if the suspension is *latae sententiae*, his right to administer the ecclesiastical goods belonging to his position in the Church.

A censure's prohibition against celebrating the sacraments is not to be enforced when a cleric encounters a Catholic in danger of death.

This applies regardless of whether the cleric is laboring under suspension, interdict or excommunication. The law's intention is to punish the wayward cleric, not the individual Catholic who requires the sacraments in an emergency.

74. What are expiatory penalties? How do they differ from medicinal penalties?

Expiatory penalties, unlike medicinal penalties, are intended to restore order by punishing the offender. Whereas the offender has the right to have a censure removed once he or she repents, an expiatory penalty can be imposed for a predetermined or undetermined length of time (canon 1336). For example, a religious sister might be barred from a particular residence for a year, or she might be barred until the diocesan bishop feels the situation that led to the expiatory penalty has sufficiently blown over.

Expiatory penalties are as diverse as the offenses that give rise to them. An expiatory penalty can prohibit the offender from taking up residence at a certain location or in a certain geographical area, or the penalty can limit an offender to a certain residence. This applies to both clergy and religious. The ordinary of the place where a cleric or religious is being exiled must consent (canon 1337).

An expiatory penalty can remove an offender's power to exercise orders within the Church—that is, the power that comes with ordination to the diaconate, priesthood or episcopate. An expiatory penalty can also remove an offender's office, rights, privileges, functions, titles and even honors within the Church. It can force an individual to transfer to another position of authority within the Church—for example, from pastor of a large parish to a desk job somewhere.

Finally, in the most serious cases, a cleric might find himself dismissed from the clerical state. This has become the common expiatory penalty in the United States for clergy who sexually abuse minors (see chapter eleven).

75. What are penal warnings and penances?

Penal warnings and penances are similar to expiatory penalties but much less severe. In fact, they are intended to stop small problems from developing into larger problems requiring expiatory penalties and censures. Thus a penal warning becomes appropriate when the ordinary believes that a person may be on the verge of committing an offense or has committed an offense (canon 1339).

The ordinary should warn or correct an individual in a manner that is appropriate to the individual. The ordinary must keep a record of the warning in the secret archive of the curia, the diocesan chancery office, in case proof is required at a later date.

A penance, when imposed outside of the sacrament of confession, requires the offender to perform an act of religion, piety or charity (canon 1340). For example, a Catholic caught stealing from a parish food bank might be required to pray for the homeless at the diocesan soup kitchen.

An offender should never receive a public penance if his or her offense is not publicly known. The ordinary, if he judges it to be appropriate, may add penances to his penal warnings.

76. How does the Church apply penalties in response to a particular transgression?

First of all, the ordinary must start a judicial or administrative process. He should do so only when it becomes clear to him that no other means of fraternal correction are possible or that the alleged crime is too serious to handle in a less formal fashion (canon 1341).

Ecclesiastical judges are given a certain amount of flexibility within the judicial process. For example, if the law gives the judge a choice between imposing and not imposing a specific penalty for a certain infraction, he is free to lighten the specific penalty or substitute a penance (canon 1343).

Similarly, canon 1344 allows a judge to defer the offender's punishment until a later time; not impose the recommended penalty or impose a less serious penalty when the offender has repented and done his or her best to correct the situation; not impose a penalty or impose a less severe penalty when the judge believes the civil authorities will adequately punish the offender; and take into account the fact of a first-time offense when the person has previously abided by Church law.

An ecclesiastical judge also can use alternative means of correcting a situation when the offender acts out of drunkenness or the heat of passion or has some other impediment to clear thinking at the time of the offense (canon 1345). For example, a judge may give an alcoholic the option to seek treatment, or the easily riled individual the choice to attend an anger management course.

An ecclesiastical authority cannot impose a censure unless he first gives the offender a warning and sufficient time to repent (canon 1347). This warning is required for validity and not just for lawfulness. Nor should a judge impose censures and heavier penalties unless the offense is serious enough to warrant them (canon 1349). For example, most Catholics agree that molesting children deserves dismissal from the clerical state; the same penalty would be grossly disproportional if the priest's offense was an occasional relapse into alcoholism.

Finally, the Church does not wish any of her faithful to depart from this earth without the comfort of the sacraments. Therefore, when an offender faces the danger of death, any penalty barring him from the sacraments or sacramentals is suspended for as long as the danger persists (canon 1352).

77. What are offenses against religion and the unity of the Church?

Offenses against religion and the unity of the Church are offenses that directly harm the Church. For example, schism, heresy and apostasy are among the three most serious offenses against the Catholic faith. The schismatic refuses to subject himself to the Roman pontiff or to maintain communion with those subject to the Holy Father; the heretic, having been baptized into the faith, obstinately denies or doubts a truth that must be believed as of divine and Catholic faith; and the apostate totally renounces Christ and the Christian faith.

Canon 1364 automatically excommunicates each of the aforementioned individuals. Additionally the canon permits the competent ecclesiastical authority to add other penalties, including dismissal from the clerical state when a deacon, priest or bishop commits the offense.

Excommunication automatically comes into effect when an individual commits a sacrilege against the Blessed Sacrament—either by throwing away the sacred species or by desecrating the Blessed Sacrament. This *latae sententiae* excommunication is reserved to the Holy See, meaning that only the Holy See can remove it (canon 1367). Canon 1367 allows for additional penalties, including dismissal from the clerical state when the offender is a cleric.

Other offenses against religion and the unity of the Church include participation in religious ceremonies prohibited by the Church (canon 1365), allowing one's children to be baptized or raised in a religion other than the Catholic faith (canon 1366), perjury before a competent ecclesiastical authority (canon 1368) and public blasphemy against the Church's teaching on faith and morals (canon 1369).

78. What are offenses against ecclesiastical authorities and the freedom of the Church?

These are actions and words that unduly harm the Church's lawful leaders or restrict the Church's freedom. Historically penalties were attached to these offenses as a means of offering clergy and religious some protection, since canon law forbade clergy from carrying weapons. These types of offenses are outlined in canons 1370 to 1377.

Canon 1370 imposes an automatic excommunication upon any individual who physically attacks the Holy Father. Other penalties may be added if the offender is a cleric. If the victim is a bishop, then the canon imposes an automatic interdict, as well as a suspension if the offender is another cleric. (Of course, there's an unwritten exception to this law in Canada when bishops, priests and seminarians square off in a hockey game.) Finally, the canon prescribes "a just penalty" for those who physically attack a cleric or religious out of hatred for the Church, her hierarchy or the Catholic faith.

Canon 1371 has changed since it first appeared in the 1983 *Code of Canon Law*. Pope John Paul II expanded this canon in his apostolic letter *Ad Tuendam Fidem* in 1998. The canon now requires "a just penalty" for those who, despite having been warned, teach doctrine condemned by the Holy Father or by an ecumenical council, as well as those who obstinately reject the Church's teaching on faith and morals. The canon does not define "just penalty." This omission is deliberate, in that it allows the lawful ecclesiastical authority the necessary discretion to correct the situation. The same law applies to an individual who, despite a canonical warning, continues to disobey the Holy See, his or her ordinary or his or her lawful superior.[1]

Canon 1372 requires the imposition of a censure when an individual appeals to an ecumenical council to judge the actions of the Holy Father. Canon 1373 requires an interdict or some other just penalty should a person incite his or her fellow Catholics to hate the Holy See or an ordinary.

Other offenses against ecclesiastical authorities and the freedom of the Church include being a member of an association that conspires against the Church (canon 1374), unlawfully hindering a minister in the exercise of his ministry (canon 1375), profaning a sacred object (canon 1376) and confiscating or taking without proper permission assets belonging to the Church (canon 1377).

79. What are offenses against special obligations?

Clergy and religious devote their lives to God and to ministry to God's people. While this creates a situation in which the clergy and religious enjoy a certain respect, it also creates some special obligations. Great harm can come to the Church when a cleric or religious violates a special obligation.

One such obligation is that of abstaining from holding political office. For example, many Catholics from Canada were scandalized in the fall of 2006 by the actions of Father Raymond Gravel. The priest, who had previously dissented in public from the Church's teachings on homosexuality and abortion, ran for a seat in the Canadian legislature.

He was elected a member of the Bloc Québécois, which is Quebec's separatist party. As you can imagine, this outraged both orthodox Catholics and patriotic Canadians.

Canon 1392 prohibits clergy and religious from engaging in business practices that are contrary to the code. Of course, a married permanent deacon still has to earn a living, so the code recognizes exceptions for permanent deacons. Nevertheless, the general principle is that clergy and religious dedicate themselves to the service of the Christian faithful.

Clergy are often bound by their ecclesiastical office to reside in a certain location. For example, a diocesan bishop is bound to reside in his diocese. Canon 1396 allows for the punishment of an individual who violates a canonical obligation of residence.

The most obvious obligation of a cleric is that of celibacy and continence. Canon 1394 automatically suspends a cleric who tries to marry, even if the intended marriage is only civil. Archbishop Emmanuel Milingo is probably the most well-known recent individual to fall under this penalty. The Zambian archbishop created an international stir when he attempted marriage in a mass wedding ceremony before the controversial religious leader Reverend Moon. Archbishop Milingo faced an automatic suspension of his priestly faculties. If the person attempting marriage is not a cleric but a religious in perpetual vows, then canon 1394 automatically imposes an interdict.

Canon 1395 prescribes a suspension for a cleric who lives with, or is involved with, a sexual partner without attempting to marry. The canon also allows the punishment of clerics for other sins against sexual morality, depending upon their severity.

Canon 1378 automatically excommunicates a priest who absolves, through the sacrament of confession, his partner in a sexual sin (see canon 977). The removal of this excommunication is reserved to the Holy See. The purpose of this canon is clear: It helps prevent a priest from abusing his priesthood by absolving his partner after engaging in illicit sexual relations. This is among the more serious crimes a priest can commit, and it is taken most seriously when the priest also uses the confessional to lure his partner into illicit sexual relations (canon 1387). In fact, the *Code of Canon Law* demands dismissal from the clerical state in the most serious cases.

The sacramental seal, as most Catholics know, is inviolable. Christ's faithful approach the sacrament of penance to share their most deeply held sins and to receive Christ's forgiveness. Thus their confidence in the secrecy of confession must be absolute. Canon 1388 severely punishes a priest who violates the seal of confession. If the violation is direct—that is, if the priest reveals to a third party the identity of the penitent and the contents of a penitent's confession— then the penalty is automatic excommunication reserved to the Holy See. The canon also punishes interpreters and translators who violate the seal of confession.

These violations of the integrity of the sacrament of penance are among those Pope John Paul II identified as "grave delicts" in his 2001 apostolic letter *Sacramentorum Sanctitatis Tutela*. The Holy See has the authority to prosecute such offenses (see chapter eleven).

80. How does the Church discipline persons who minister beyond their rank of holy orders?

Because of the great trust and respect that Catholics place in their clergy, it is not unusual for unscrupulous men to impersonate clergy in public or for a disgraced cleric to try and continue ministering outside of the Church's boundaries. Hence the need for the Church to protect Catholics from those who would usurp ecclesiastical office.

Canon 1378 imposes an automatic interdict or suspension upon one who attempts to celebrate the Eucharist while not an ordained priest and one who attempts to administer the sacrament of confession while unable to absolve. Depending upon the gravity of the situation, the offender may receive additional penalties—including excommunication.

The purpose of canon 1378 is clear. The sacraments are the center of a Catholic's spiritual life. Catholics must feel confident that the sacraments are valid. Canon 1379 prescribes a just penalty for any other case in which a person impersonates the administrator of a sacrament.

Other offenses in this category include simony (canon 1380), usurping or unlawfully retaining an ecclesiastical office (canon 1381), ordaining another bishop or superior's subject without a proper dimissorial letter (canon 1383), unlawfully exercising sacred ministry (canon 1384), trafficking in Mass intentions (canon 1385), abusing ecclesiastical office and culpable negligence (canon 1389).

One of the most serious crimes in this category is the consecration of a bishop without a papal mandate. Hence canon 1382 automatically excommunicates both the bishop who presides over the unlawful consecration and the bishop who receives unlawful consecration. Because of the gravity of the offense, only the Holy See can lift this *latae sententiae* (automatic) excommunication. We've already noted the example of Archbishop Lefebvre's excommunication (see question 10).

81. What is the offense of falsehood?

Falsehood is an offense against the eighth commandment, namely, "Neither shall you bear false witness against your neighbor." This commandment is often simplified to "Thou shalt not lie." Catholics must be able to trust one another in carrying out Christ's work. Using words deceptively undermines trust among Christ's faithful and, in many cases, brings great harm to the Church and to fellow Christians.

Probably the most harmful offense in this category is what canonists call "false denunciation." This occurs when an individual falsely accuses a priest of having sexually solicited him or her in the confessional, one of the most serious crimes a priest can commit (see questions 79 and 84). A priest is still bound to the seal of confession when responding to the allegation. This makes it difficult for him to defend himself against this charge.

For this reason canon 1390 imposes an automatic interdict on a false accuser. When the false denunciation is perpetuated by another cleric, then that cleric's penalty is suspension. Additionally, canon 1390 prescribes a just penalty for other calumnious denunciations of an individual before his or her superior.

Additional crimes of falsehood for which the code permits a just penalty are authoring a false ecclesiastical document or unlawfully altering a legitimate one, using a false or altered document for business related to the Church and making false assertions within a Church document intended for public use.

82. What are offenses against human life and liberty?

Offenses against human life and liberty are those that do unjust physical violence to another individual. Canon 1397 lists the following as offenses of this nature: murder, abduction, imprisonment, mutilation and inflicting a grave wound. The canon prescribes that the offender be punished according to the gravity of his or her actions. Thus the mutilation of another person's entire leg should be treated more seriously than the mutilation of a single toe, provided all other circumstances are equal.

Abortion is one of the most serious offenses against human life, since abortion is intrinsically evil and the child in the womb is among the most defenseless of human life. Canon 1398 imposes an automatic excommunication on those who actually procure an abortion, provided no diminishing causes are present.

CHAPTER ELEVEN

Safeguarding the Sanctity of the Sacraments

83. Does the Vatican intervene in situations where there is lack of respect for the sacraments?

The Church refers to the most serious religious offenses that a person can commit as *delicts*. The 1983 *Code of Canon Law* already reserved a number of these offenses for consideration by the Vatican offices, and Pope John Paul II increased the number in 2001 with *Sacramentorum Sanctitatis Tutela* ("Safeguarding the Sanctity of the Sacraments"). This document and its accompanying norms, commonly referred to as *Graviora Delicta* (meaning "grave delicts"), transfers to the Apostolic See (Congregation for the Doctrine of the Faith) the authority to prosecute certain offenses relating to the Eucharist, penance and the sixth commandment of the Decalogue.

Violations in these matters affect the whole Church. In some parts of the world, small dioceses in mission territories do not have the means to conduct trials. Referring the most serious offenses to the Congregation for the Doctrine of the Faith allows bishops to treat such matters expeditiously.

Even though the diocesan bishop now must report certain matters to the Congregation for the Doctrine of the Faith, he is still very engaged in the process of investigating such matters. It remains the bishop's responsibility to make a preliminary investigation into allegations of these delicts before sending notice to the Apostolic See. In fact, the Congregation may even refer the case back to the bishop for a trial, with the Congregation serving as the court of appeal.

If a bishop is asked to conduct a penal trial on behalf of the Congregation, the procedure as outlined in the 1983 *Code of Canon Law* must be followed. Normally only priests can fulfill the roles of judge, promotor of justice, notary and advocate in these cases; however, the Apostolic See has granted permission for lay people to assume some of these functions in particular cases. The content of the allegation and the acts (the record) of a trial are treated with secrecy; however, the outcome of a trial can be made known to the public.

84. What constitutes offenses against the Eucharist and the sacrament of penance?

Graviora Delicta identifies five offenses that relate to the Blessed Sacrament and four offenses that relate to the sacrament of reconciliation:

The Blessed Sacrament: (1) any action that gravely offends the Eucharist—for example, using it for a sacrilegious purpose or throwing it away (also see canon 1367); (2) the action of attempting to celebrate the Mass by one who is not ordained to the priesthood (also see canons 1378, paragraph 2, and 1379); (3) simulation of a liturgical celebration of the Eucharist; (4) celebrating the Eucharist with a minister of an ecclesial community (that is, Christian denomination) that does not enjoy apostolic succession and does not recognize the sacramental dignity of priestly ordination (also see canons 908 and 1365); (5) consecration, for sacrilegious purposes, of only one of the eucharistic elements or consecration of both outside the Mass (also see canon 927).

Penance: (1) absolving a partner for a sexual offense committed with that person (also see canons 977 and 1378, paragraph 1); (2) solicitation by a priest of behavior of a sexual nature while in confession or under the pretext of confession (also see canon 1387); (3) direct or indirect violation of the sacramental seal of confession (it should be noted that the delict of indirectly violating the sacramental seal was added to the list by the pope on February 7, 2003; also see canon 1388, paragraph 1); (4) transmitting or recording what is said in confession by the confessor or the penitent (a delict that the pope also added on February 7, 2003). [1]

A person must be Catholic (Latin or Eastern) for a delict to apply. If a non-Catholic were to commit such offenses, there would be no canonical crime, and the Church would not claim jurisdiction over the case.

Those who do not possess the use of reason cannot commit or be punished for a delict (canon 1322). As well, those who are under the age of sixteen, are ignorant of the fact that they are violating a law or are acting under physical force, grave fear or in self-defense cannot be punished for a delict (canon 1323). When clerics are involved (that is, deacons, priests and bishops), it is fair to presume that unless subjected to physical force, grave fear or self-defense, the offender is subject to a penalty.

Some of these offenses involve only clerics. Since only priests and bishops can consecrate the Eucharist, numbers 2, 4 and 5 under the heading "Blessed Sacrament" would apply only to them. Since only priests and bishops can celebrate the sacrament of penance validly, delicts 1, 2 and 3 under the heading "Penance" apply only to them.

85. What constitutes offenses against the sixth commandment?

Offenses against the sixth commandment ("Thou shalt not commit adultery") are sexual in nature. Canon 1395, paragraph 1 states that "a cleric living in concubinage" or committing "some other external sin against the sixth commandment of the Decalogue" is to be punished with suspension or even dismissal from the clerical state. Section 2 of canon 1395 allows for an increase in the degree of punishment if the delict was committed by force, by threats, in public or with a minor under the age of sixteen.

Sacramentorum Sanctitatis Tutela and the accompanying norms, *Graviora Delicta*, refer only to delicts against the sixth commandment committed by a cleric with a minor—that is, someone under the age of eighteen. All other cases of a delict in violation of the sixth commandment, if not treated in *Graviora Delicta* under the heading "Eucharist" or "Penance," do not have to be brought to the attention of the Congregation for the Doctrine of the Faith.

It should be noted that many conferences of bishops have taken it upon themselves to devise their own definitions of what might constitute a violation of the sixth commandment. In 1992 the Canadian Conference of Catholic Bishops reported that such sexual offenses may be defined as "contacts or interactions between a child and an adult when the child is being used as an object of sexual gratification for the adult." The conference went on to explain, "A child is abused whether or not this activity involves explicit force, whether or not it involves genital or physical contact, whether or not it is initiated by the child, and whether or not there is discernible harmful outcome."[2] This definition was not issued as a canonical, legal definition for the processing of cases of abuse. It was made as part of a report by an Ad hoc committee on sexual abuse of the Canadian Conference of Catholic Bishops.

The United States Conference of Catholic Bishops, in their 2005 document entitled "Essential Norms for Diocesan/Eparchial Policies Dealing With Allegations of Sexual Abuse of Minors by Priests and Deacons," did not utilize this broad definition of abuse. The 2005 Norms defer to the definition in canon 1395 that cases of external, objectively grave violations are considered by the norms.

In any case, it would seem that whenever an external manifestation of sexual behavior with a minor under the age of eighteen occurs— even without contact with the minor, as in cases of pornography—the local bishop must refer the matter to the Congregation for the Doctrine of the Faith when it involves a cleric.

86. What role does a conference of bishops take in considering offenses that violate the sixth commandment?

Each conference of bishops has the prerogative to propose changes to the universal laws of the Church in order to make them fit better the circumstances of their country or countries. The *Code of Canon Law* provides instances that mandate the bishops to go ahead and make alterations, which subsequently the Apostolic See reviews for its approval. There are, however, truly exceptional circumstances that warrant other more creative ways of adapting the law where a mandate within the *Code of Canon Law* is not provided.

Such was the case on June 14, 2002, when the United States Conference of Catholic Bishops devised its norms for handling cases of sexual abuse of minors by priests and deacons. The bishops sent these to the Apostolic See. The Congregation for Bishops approved them on December 8, 2002. The USCCB revised the norms in June 2005 and the Congregation of Bishops approved them on May 5, 2006.

The so-called "Dallas Norms" are novel on a number of fronts. They oblige every bishop in the United States to implement in his diocese a policy for handling cases of sexual abuse of minors by clergy. They also oblige the bishops to supply staff people to respond to those who might make a disclosure of abuse. Every diocese must have a review board, composed of a majority of laypeople, who advise the bishop on allegations and on an accused person's suitability for ministry and who review the diocesan policy regarding such matters.

The Dallas Norms state that in cases where the abuse is admitted or is determined by a penal trial or administrative process—even for a single instance of abuse of a minor—if the priest has not been dismissed from the clerical state, he will be removed permanently from public ministry. The norms allow the bishop to approach the Congregation for the Doctrine of the Faith to remove the period of prescription (see question 97) in individual cases and to use an administrative process to remove the offending cleric from office or to restrict his faculties. This last point was a particularly bold move, since the 1983 *Code of Canon Law* removed the possibility of permanent leave through administrative processes.

Finally, among other things, the Dallas Norms mandate a system of background checks concerning any information indicating the priest or deacon may be a danger to children or young people, when the priest or deacon moves from one diocese to another to perform public ministry. The United States Conference of Catholic Bishops facilitates a national review board, which audits dioceses annually for their compliance with these norms.

87. Is there a statute of limitation in Church law concerning delicts that violate the sixth commandment?

There is a statute of limitation on crimes in Church law, but it is called *prescription*. Prescription is the period between when the delict occurred and when the offender can no longer be tried and punished for it.

One might think that it is not right for the law to allow someone to be exempt from punishment for a crime; however, like civil law, there is a concern that, with the passage of time, the quality and availability of evidence diminish and the possibility of a wrong judgment increases.

In a 2001 address to cardinals of the United States, Pope John Paul II stated, "People need to know that there is no place in the priesthood and religious life for those who would harm the young."[3] Though there is a period of prescription in Church law, there is also a recognition that the Church needs to protect God's children from harm.

The *Code of Canon Law* imposes a five-year period of prescription for *all* delicts. The 2001 document *Graviora Delicta* increased the period of prescription for *sexual abuse* of a minor to ten years from the minor's eighteenth birthday. *Graviora Delicta* also increased the period of prescription for delicts against the *Eucharist* and *penance* to ten years from the date of the offense (*Graviora Delicta*, 5).

These aspects of prescription are certainly not meant to confuse the situation and discourage someone from disclosing information concerning the abuse of minors—or abuse of anyone for that matter. The prescription refers to the possibility of a Church trial to determine guilt and impose a penalty, and even if the period of prescription has expired, certain administrative procedures can be used to restrict errant clerics and even bar them from ministry. Again, practice has shown that the period of prescription will not stand in the way of imposing restrictions on ministry in order to protect minors and preserve the integrity of the priesthood and the Church's mission.

88. Will an allegation of sexual abuse always result in a trial?

When the ordinary receives an allegation of sexual abuse of a minor by a cleric, he is to initiate a preliminary investigation either personally or through a delegate. The preliminary investigation seeks to identify whether or not the allegation has a semblance of truth. Once a positive determination has been made, the ordinary no longer has any competence to handle the case. There is some gray area concerning this criterion of "semblance of truth;" however, the practice in recent years has been to err on the side of caution and to send cases to the Congregation for the Doctrine of the Faith, in accordance with the direction Pope John Paul II gave *Sacramentorum Sanctitatis Tutela*.

89. What happens after a preliminary investigation determines that an allegation of sexual abuse of a minor appears true?

When the Congregation for the Doctrine of the Faith receives an allegation of sexual abuse of a minor by a cleric, the first thing that it determines is whether or not the standard of a "semblance of truth" was reached in the preliminary investigation. As well, the Congregation verifies that all the appropriate procedures were observed in preparing the preliminary investigation. The Congregation may ask for more information concerning the case before these matters can be decided. If the Congregation is confident that the allegation has credibility, it can choose from among a number of ways to proceed.[4]

If the Congregation determines that no further evidence is required and that an administrative process or penal trial would not add anything to the case, the Congregation can dismiss the cleric administratively from the clerical state. The cleric then can appeal the decision to a higher level within the Congregation.

The Congregation may also ask the accused cleric to seek dispensation voluntarily from all the obligations arising from ordination—that is, that he assume the day-to-day life of a layperson. If the cleric refuses, the Congregation can present the case to the pope for a forced dismissal of the cleric, and no decision of the pope can be appealed.

The Congregation can also elect to return a case to the diocesan bishop, who can then collect more evidence, consider the merits of the case and offer his opinion to the Congregation. The Congregation would then decide whether or not to impose a penalty, a decision that the cleric can appeal only to a higher level within the Congregation.

The Congregation may elect to return the case to the diocesan bishop for a penal trial, which must unfold in accordance with the steps set forth in the *Code of Canon Law* (canons 1311–1399). This process is reserved for more questionable allegations, where more evidence is needed. The cleric gets an opportunity to defend himself. The penal trial requires at least three judges, a promotor of justice, notaries, one or more advocates and so on. The result, along with the trial documents, must be forwarded to the Congregation for the Doctrine of the Faith. The first decision of guilty or not guilty can be appealed to the Congregation. Once the Congregation decides the matter on appeal, it becomes a settled matter, referred to as *res iudicata,* "a thing decided."

90. How can a priest be dismissed from the clerical state but still remain a priest?

It is the theology of the Church that when a man is ordained to the diaconate, priesthood or episcopacy, there is a change in him that no human power can undo. It may be argued that some persons were never validly ordained, but these cases are rare and usually relate to an aspect of the ordination ceremony or to the fact that the ordination was not performed by one able to ordain. The phrase "Once a priest, always a priest" is accurate.

Though the analogy has fault, we can liken removing a priest from ministry to removing a doctor from his practice of medicine. The physician will always possess his academic credentials, and more importantly his fundamental outlook on life will always be that of a physician. In the same way, a priest remains a priest even when he no longer functions as one.

There are two sanctions or penalties that apply to clerics who have been found guilty of sexually abusing minors. The more severe course of action is to dismiss a priest from the clerical state. Dismissal is removal of all the rights and privileges that the man had to conduct ministry in the name of the Catholic Church. He must return to a way of life like that of a layperson: Although he maintains his status as a Catholic who can go to Mass and receive the sacraments, he is usually restricted from assuming any role of leadership or ministry in the Church. Again, he is still a priest, but he may not function as one. Dismissal is the most severe course of disciplinary action that can be taken against a cleric.

The other way to remove a cleric from ministry is to impose on him a permanent leave. This administrative process is not available to bishops in all parts of the world. The United States, in drafting its own norms for treating such matters, obtained permission to utilize this method. The cleric is not dismissed from the clerical state, but he may not present himself as a cleric or perform public ministry. In the cases of priests, about the only function they may continue that is proper to ordination is to celebrate Mass privately.

91. What financial obligations does a diocese have toward a priest who has been removed from ministry?

In recent years cases of clerical sexual abuse of minors have come to light in large numbers, and many of the allegations date back decades. Some of the accused clerics are retired and drawing a pension. When these individuals are removed from ministry by way of dismissal from the clerical state or permanent leave, if their Church pensions and government programs such as Social Security do not continue to meet their needs they may need to find employment.

But what is a bishop to do with a priest who is removed or voluntarily leaves before his pension matures? What does a bishop do in the case of a middle-aged priest who is beyond his years for retraining or perhaps belongs to a small diocese where he could not get a job because people do not trust him? Is the bishop's duty toward those on permanent leave different from his duty toward those dismissed from the clerical state?

We realize that this book is supposed to be answering questions rather than asking them, but the solutions to these matters still are evolving, and there is no uniform practice among dioceses throughout the world. There are a number of distinctions that can be proposed:

- *Remuneration.* An active cleric, a cleric on sabbatical leave or a cleric on medical leave has a right to remuneration that befits his condition (canon 281).
- *Sustenance.* A cleric who is taking a voluntary temporary leave or involuntary permanent leave has the right to be cared for by the diocese or institute in which he is incardinated, since the Church has a duty to care for its clerics. Such clerics do not deserve remuneration, since they are doing nothing to warrant remuneration.

Even providing sustenance can be extremely burdensome financially for a diocese. In the event that such individuals find alternate means of employment, the diocese no longer needs to supply such sustenance.

- *Equitable and just separation.* A diocese or religious order does not need to care for a cleric who has been dismissed from the clerical state. Nonetheless, when and if they are dismissed, equity would seem to dictate that such individuals have the right to some sort of "severance pay," medical assistance or job retraining allowance. This last item, however, is not confirmed in law and is the opinion of the authors.

CHAPTER TWELVE

The Code of Canons of the Eastern Churches

92. What are the Eastern Churches? Do they have their own code of canon law?

Many people, particularly Westerners, view the Roman Catholic Church as a rigid hierarchy. This is far from the case. The Roman Catholic Church is actually a communion of twenty-three Churches *sui iuris* ("of one's own right"), an expression that means that the Church enjoys a large degree of autonomy while still preserving full communion. By far the largest *sui iuris* Church is the Latin Church, of which the bishop of Rome is the visible head and for which the Code of Canon Law was promulgated.

The other twenty-two Churches *sui iuris* are known as Eastern Catholic Churches. Members of these *sui iuris* Churches have their own code of canon law. That code, promulgated in 1990, is known by English-speaking canonists as the Code of Canons of the Eastern Churches or sometimes as the Code of Canons of the Oriental Churches. Canonists often refer to this code by its Latin acronym *CCEO* (*Codex Canonum Ecclesiarum Orientalium*).

The twenty-two Eastern Catholic Churches covered by the *CCEO* fall into five major spiritual and liturgical traditions:

Alexandrian Tradition:
- Coptic Catholic Church
- Ethiopic Catholic Church

Antiochian Tradition:
- Maronite Church
- Syrian Catholic Church
- Syro-Malankara Catholic Church

Armenian Tradition:
- Armenian Catholic Church

Chaldean or East Syrian Tradition:
- Chaldean Catholic Church
- Syro-Malabar Catholic Church

Byzantine or Constantinople Tradition:
- Albanian Byzantine Catholic Church
- Belarusian Greek Catholic Church
- Bulgarian Greek Catholic Church
- Byzantine Church of the Eparchy of Kriĭevci
- Greek Byzantine Catholic Church
- Hungarian Greek Catholic Church
- Italo-Albanian Catholic Church
- Macedonian Greek Catholic Church
- Melkite Greek Catholic Church
- Romanian Catholic Church
- Russian Byzantine Catholic Church
- Ruthenian Catholic Church
- Slovak Greek Catholic Church
- Ukrainian Catholic Church

A Catholic belonging to any of these *sui iuris* Churches is subject to the *CCEO* rather than the Latin code. Yet each of these traditions is as unique as the Latin liturgical and spiritual tradition to which Catholics in the West adhere. By far the largest of these traditions is the Byzantine.

The Macedonian Greek Catholic hierarchy was only recently re-established. Therefore some sources still number the Eastern Catholic Churches at twenty-one, having not yet taken the Macedonian Church into account. Additionally, the Church is currently working with Georgian Catholics and Czech Catholics to reestablish their respective hierarchies. Therefore it is possible the number of Eastern Catholics could increase to twenty-four in the near future.

93. How is the *CCEO* different from the Latin code?

While the *CCEO* and the Latin code have a lot in common, there is much that is distinctive in each. One of the first differences one sees is their overall structure.

The Latin code is divided into seven books that express the Church's three functions—teaching, sanctifying and governing—within the traditional Roman legal categories. The *CCEO*, on the other hand, begins with six preliminary canons. These canons establish the Eastern code's legal scope, stating that the *CCEO* applies only to Eastern Catholics and that it does not impact upon particular agreements into which the Holy See has entered. Further, these preliminary canons establish when the *CCEO* will take precedence over contrary laws.

Another 1534 canons follow these six preliminary ones, for a total of 1540 *CCEO* canons. The remaining canons are grouped under thirty titles. These titles, and the canons they cover, are as follows:

Title 1: The Rights and Obligations of All the Christian Faithful (canons 7 to 26)

Title 2: Churches *Sui Iuris* and Rites (canons 27 to 41)

Title 3: The Supreme Authority of the Church (canons 42 to 54)

Title 4: The Patriarchal Churches (canons 55 to 150)

Title 5: The Major Archiepiscopal Churches (canons 151 to 154)

Title 6: Metropolitan Churches and Other Churches *Sui Iuris* (canons 155 to 176)

Title 7: Eparchies and Bishops (canons 177 to 310)

Title 8: Exarchies and Exarchs (canons 311 to 321)

Title 9: Assemblies of Hierarchs of Several Churches *Sui Iuris* (canon 322)

Title 10: Clergy (canons 323 to 398)

Title 11: Laypersons (canons 399 to 409)

Title 12: Monks and Other Religious as Well as Members of Other Institutes of Consecrated Life (canons 410 to 572)

Title 13: Associations of the Christian Faithful (canons 573 to 583)

Title 14: Evangelization of Nations (canons 584 to 594)

Title 15: The Ecclesiastical Magisterium (canons 595 to 666)

Title 16: Divine Worship and Especially the Sacraments (canons 667 to 895)

94. What is a patriarchal Church, as understood by the CCEO? What is a patriarch?

The CCEO devotes title 4 to patriarchal Churches. Beginning with CCEO canon 55, the Eastern Code recognizes this ancient practice within the universal Church whereby the head of certain *sui iuris* Eastern Churches is honored with the title "patriarch." Thus a patriarch is a bishop whose authority—spiritually, canonically and historically—extends over all the other bishops and faithful of his *sui iuris* Church (CCEO, canon 56).

Patriarchs of the Eastern Churches take precedence over all other bishops, Latin and Eastern, with the exception of the bishop of Rome (CCEO, canon 58). Among themselves the patriarchs are equal in dignity; however, they enjoy a precedence of honor in the following order, as outlined in CCEO, canon 59:

Patriarch of Constantinople
Patriarch of Alexandria

> Patriarch of Antioch
> Patriarch of Jerusalem

All other patriarchs according to the historical order in which their see was founded, starting with the earliest.

Occasionally historical circumstances will create a situation in which more than one patriarch lays claim to a title. For example, there are five patriarchs who, due to schisms within the early Church, claim the title "patriarch of Antioch." As of this writing three of these patriarchs lead *sui iuris* Churches in full communion with Rome: His Beatitude Ignace Pierre VIII Abdel-Ahad, Syrian Catholic Church; His Beatitude Nasrallah Pierre Cardinal Sfeir, Maronite Catholic Church; and His Beatitude Gregory III Laham, Melkite Catholic Church. The Church recognizes the patriarchal title of all three men. Should they gather together, their precedence of honor would descend according to the order in which each man became patriarch of his respective *sui iuris* Church.

95. How does a bishop become patriarch of his Church *sui iuris*?

Patriarchs, like popes, are elected. In fact, patriarchal elections are not unlike papal elections.

The patriarchal Church's synod of bishops gathers within a month of the previous patriarch's resigning from office or passing away (*CCEO* canon 63). Two-thirds of the synod's bishops must be present for the patriarchal election to be valid (*CCEO* canon 69). *CCEO* canon 72 requires the patriarch-elect to receive two-thirds of the synod's vote. Nevertheless, a *sui iuris* Church's particular law can allow for an absolute majority (over 50 percent) after the third ballot. While only the synod's bishops can vote for the new patriarch, they are free to elect someone other than their own.

Should the synod elect a bishop, the patriarchal Church can enthrone him immediately following his acceptance of the election. If the patriarch-elect is not a bishop, however, he must receive episcopal consecration before being enthroned as patriarch (*CCEO* canon 75).

Following a patriarch's enthronement, the synod of bishops must write a letter to the supreme pontiff and the patriarchs of the other *sui iuris* Churches. This letter should state that the new patriarch was elected and enthroned and that the synod witnessed the new patriarch's profession of faith and his promise of fidelity in carrying out his duties as patriarch (*CCEO* canon 76). Additionally, the new patriarch must address and personally sign a letter to the supreme pontiff requesting full communion.

96. What canonical authority does a patriarch possess within his *sui iuris* Church?

CCEO canon 77 details the functions and authority that come with being patriarch of a *sui iuris* Church. A patriarch's authority within his *sui iuris* Church is not merely honorific. He possesses actual power that he can wield when necessary. This authority is ordinary, meaning it comes with the title *patriarch*, and it is proper, meaning he has every right to exercise this power.

This authority is also personal, which means that the patriarch cannot always delegate his power, nor can he appoint a vicar over his entire *sui iuris* Church (*CCEO* canon 78). Of course, a patriarch's jurisdiction generally is limited to his *sui iuris* Church.

That being said, *CCEO* canon 82 explains that a patriarch has the authority to decree how the law should be observed within his *sui iuris* Church; to instruct members of his *sui iuris* Church in doctrine, piety, the correction of abuses and approved and recommended spiritual practices; to publish encyclical letters pertaining to issues affecting his *sui iuris* Church; and to require all the clergy and consecrated members within his *sui iuris* Church—including other bishops—to make public his decrees, instructions and encyclicals. When an issue is serious, however, the patriarch must consult his *sui iuris* Church's permanent synod, synod of bishops or patriarchal assembly—that is, the patriarchs of all the other patriarchal Churches.

Additionally, *CCEO* canon 86 states that a patriarch is competent to ordain and enthrone the metropolitan bishops of his *sui iuris*

Church and, in some *sui iuris* Churches, the other bishops as well. A patriarch may ordain and enthrone a bishop of his *sui iuris* Church whom the Roman pontiff has appointed for service outside of the patriarchal Church's territorial boundaries. Take, for example, a Melkite Catholic bishop appointed to a diocese in the United States or Canada. Once the patriarch has carried out the ordination and enthronement, he must notify the Holy See as quickly as possible.

97. Are all Eastern Catholic Churches patriarchal Churches?

Not all *sui iuris* Churches are patriarchal. One also finds, among the Eastern Catholic Churches, major archiepiscopal Churches, metropolitan Churches and Churches that are overseen by a hierarch.

Major archiepiscopal Churches are overseen by a major archbishop. Because of their similarity to patriarchal Churches, the CCEO summarizes the topic in canons 151 to 155. A major archbishop possesses over his *sui iuris* Church most of the same powers as a patriarch. In terms of precedence, major archbishops come after patriarchs according to the historical order in which their *sui iuris* Church became a major archiepiscopal Church. Lastly, the election of the major archbishop differs from that of a patriarch on one key point: The Roman pontiff must approve the major archbishop's election before he can be enthroned.

A metropolitan Church is a *sui iuris* Church overseen by a metropolitan archbishop appointed by the supreme pontiff. A council of hierarchs (a council made up of bishops of a *sui iuris* Church) assists the metropolitan archbishop in his oversight (CCEO canon 155). A new metropolitan has up to three months to petition the supreme pontiff for a pallium (CCEO canon 156), which is a wool collar that symbolizes the metropolitan's authority over his *sui iuris* Church as well as the Church's full communion with Rome. Only upon receiving the pallium does the law permit the metropolitan to call together the council of hierarchs or consecrated bishops.

As with patriarchs and major archbishops, a metropolitan's authority over his *sui iuris* Church is also ordinary, proper and personal

(*CCEO* canon 157). Within his *sui iuris* metropolitan Church, *CCEO* canon 159 permits the metropolitan to ordain and enthrone bishops; call together and preside over the council of hierarchs; establish a metropolitan tribunal; ensure that the Catholic faith and Church discipline are followed; carry out canonical visitations in individual eparchies should the eparchial bishop neglect this responsibility; appoint an eparchial administrator when needed, such as when a see becomes vacant; confirm or appoint individuals to an ecclesiastical office when the eparchial bishop neglects to carry out this responsibility; and share the supreme pontiff's correspondence and other acts with the bishops and others of his *sui iuris* Church. If an issue is serious, the metropolitan and the eparchial bishops must consult with one another (*CCEO* canon 160).

Finally, *CCEO* canon 174 provides for *sui iuris* Churches that are overseen by a hierarch. Generally these *sui iuris* Churches are quite small. The Holy See appoints the hierarch, who is usually a bishop.

98. I am a Latin Catholic. My fiancé, a former atheist from the Ukraine, is a Ukrainian Catholic whom I sponsored into the Church. Why won't our bishop allow my father, a permanent deacon, to perform our wedding, as he did with my siblings?

While the Latin code generally applies only to Latin Catholics (canon 1) and the *CCEO* generally applies only to Eastern Catholics (*CCEO* canon 1), there are some exceptions to this rule. Marriage between a Latin Catholic and an Eastern Catholic is one of these exceptions. Since you are a Latin seeking to marry a Ukrainian, both codes apply.

The theology of marriage evolved separately in the East and in the West. Among Latin Catholics consent makes the marriage. This means that the couple are the ministers of the sacrament. The couple confect the sacrament of marriage when they exchange their wedding vows—that is, publicly express their consent to the marriage. The priest or deacon simply witnesses the exchange of consent on behalf of the Church.

Among Eastern Catholics, as among Eastern Orthodox, the priest is no mere witness. Although marriage in the East requires the consent of the parties, it is the priest's blessing that brings about the sacrament of marriage. Thus *CCEO* canon 828 requires that a presiding priest or bishop bless a marriage in which one of the parties is an Eastern Catholic.

Except in the most extenuating of circumstances, such as in times of persecution when a priest may not be available, the requirement of the priest's blessing is for validity. Without it there is no marriage. For this reason the Church cannot allow your father to preside over your wedding, since as a permanent deacon he lacks the rank necessary to give the priestly blessing.

That being said, there is another difficulty with your situation. You sponsored your fiancé into the Ukrainian Catholic Church, thus creating a spiritual relationship between you. While the Latin code does not prohibit a godparent from marrying a godchild, canon 811 of the *CCEO* prohibits an Eastern Catholic from marrying his or her godparent or godchild. This prohibition pertains to validity. If you wish to marry this man, you need a dispensation—that is, a relaxation of this law—from the proper Ukrainian Catholic authority.

CHAPTER THIRTEEN

Ecumenism

99. What is the Ecumenical Directory?

"Ecumenical Directory" is a shortened title often used by English-speaking canonists to refer to the Pontifical Council for Promoting Christian Unity's 1993 *Directory for the Application of Principles and Norms on Ecumenism*. The Ecumenical Directory, as its longer official title suggests, provides the Church's pastors and faithful with direction when engaging in activities with other Christians. The directory received Pope John Paul II's approval on March 25, 1993.

The Ecumenical Directory is broken down into five chapters that cover 218 articles. Chapter one, entitled "The Search for Christian Unity," covers the Church's commitment to ecumenism arising from the Second Vatican Council. Chapter two, "The Organization in the Catholic Church of the Service of Christian Unity," outlines the people and structures within the Church tasked with promoting ecumenism. Chapter three promotes "Ecumenical Formation in the Catholic Church."

Chapters four and five deal with the participation of Catholics in ecumenism. Chapter four, which goes by the title "Communion in Life and Spiritual Activity Among the Baptized," outlines when Catholics are permitted to share in prayer and other spiritual activities with non-Catholic Christians. Chapter five, "Ecumenical Cooperation, Dialogue and Common Witness," guides Catholics participating in other ecumenical activities, such as setting up a food bank with other local Christian communities and, as was seen throughout Canada during the so-called "same-sex marriage" debate, publishing a joint statement with evangelical Protestants defending the traditional definition of marriage as exclusive to one man and one woman.

The Ecumenical Directory is not law in the strict sense of the word *legislation*. Nevertheless, as an act of executive power within the Church, it is law in the broader sense of jurisprudence. Its purpose is to guide bishops, canonists, ecumenists and other Catholics in under-standing how to interpret Church law when carrying out ecumenical duties in the Church. Secondarily, it provides a clear statement to the Church's ecumenical partners of the Church's commitment to Christian unity.

Which brings us to one last point: Ecumenism pertains to prayer and religious dialogue between baptized Christians. Dialogue with any other world religion (Sikhism, Hinduism, Mormonism and so on) falls into the category of interfaith dialogue rather than ecumenism.

100. What is a diocesan ecumenical commission?

The Ecumenical Directory recommends that every diocese have its commission or office to facilitate and promote authentic ecumenical activity at the diocesan and parish levels (42). The commission should be representative of the diocese—including clergy, religious, laity and those with various areas of expertise. The commission should include representatives from the diocesan council of priests, pastoral council and diocesan and regional seminaries (43).

This ecumenical commission is tasked with helping to facilitate ecu-menism. This means that the commission should work within existing ecumenical structures where available and establish these types of structure where they are not. It also should serve as a resource to other diocesan departments, parishes, institutes of consecrated life and indi-vidual ecumenical initiatives. In short, the Ecumenical Directory envi-sions the diocesan ecumenical council as a diocesan-wide resource.

Article 44 assigns the following functions to diocesan ecumenical commissions:

1. Implement the teachings of the Second Vatican Council, Holy See, diocesan bishop and episcopal conferences on ecumenism
2. Communicate with the territorial ecumenical commission, as well as share information and experiences with the Pontifical Council for Promoting Christian Unity
3. Foster common prayer and other acts of spiritual ecumenism among Christians

4. Organize workshops, teaching seminars and lectures on ecumenism for clergy, laity, religious, seminarians and other groups within the diocese

5. Promote friendly relations with non-Catholic Christians

6. Initiate ecumenical dialogue and consultation with non-Catholic Christians

7. Help the diocese find experts at the diocesan level who can represent the Church in local ecumenical ventures

8. Promote a common Christian position on issues pertaining to education, morality, social justice, cultural issues and the arts (for example, Catholics and evangelicals often work together in the area of pro-life activism)

9. Advise the bishop as to when it would be suitable to send representatives to or receive representatives at religious events

Articles 46 and 47 recommend that the episcopal conference or synod of Eastern Catholic Churches establish a similar commission, with similar functions, at the national level.

101. What are some areas in which the Ecumenical Directory suggests cooperation between Catholics and non-Catholic Christians?

There are many areas where the Ecumenical Directory suggests possible cooperation between Catholics and non-Catholic Christians. Many of these areas are practical; they are also areas where there is already much common ground.

For example, all Christians share a love and respect for the Bible. Thus Scripture scholarship and translation offer a prime area where qualified Catholic experts can work closely with their non-Catholic Christian counterparts (183). Another area is common liturgical texts, such as the Our Father and the traditional Christian creeds (187). Additionally, Christians may want to work together on an ecumenical prayer book or hymnal.

The same is possible with catechesis (188) and missionary activity (205). In fact, as the Ecumenical Directory points out, ecumenical cooperation in missionary activity can be a missionary activity in itself, as Catholics explain to non-Catholic Christians the teachings of the Catholic faith!

Seminaries, universities, institutes of graduate studies and post-graduate research present other opportunities for Catholics to work with non-Catholic Christians (articles 191 to 203). And there are many other situations—such as prison ministry, hospital chaplaincy and the armed forces—where an ecumenical approach can benefit all (204).

There is also the possibility of ecumenical cooperation in society and culture. For example, many Christians in Germany banded together during World War II to oppose Hitler's regime from the inside. Christians can present a common Christian front when facing social and ethical issues like abortion, same-sex marriage and euthanasia (214).

Christians also can pull together resources for corporal acts of charity, such as serving the poor in developing countries, building soup kitchens for the homeless and establishing food banks for society's needy (215). This includes apostolates in the field of medicine (216), in which doctors and other medical professionals from different Christian communities can share a common Christian witness.

Finally, Catholics and non-Catholic Christians can pull together in the media to present a common Christian worldview. For example, Pete writes for *The Interim*—a Canadian pro-life newspaper supported by many different faith communities.

CONCLUSION

Coming up with an ending for a book is seldom easy. Yet we want to express our hope that this book and its predecessor will encourage your ongoing interest in canon law.

Between *Surprised by Canon Law* and *Surprised by Canon Law, Volume 2*, we have surveyed the *Code of Canon Law* and touched upon other important Church documents, like the Code of Canons of the Eastern Churches, *Pastor Bonus* and the 1993 Ecumenical Directory. These are all important pieces of legal text that guide the Church in her day-to-day affairs.

Yet covering all there is to know about canon law was not possible in these two short volumes. As you can recognize from these books, canon law is not static. It evolves as it responds to modern society and encounters new pastoral situations. As Catholics we should never forget that the law was made for us, and not we for the law. Who knows what organic development to the Church's internal legal structure we will see in the future?

Yet where the law itself might change, the principles behind it do not. Christ instituted the Church for the salvation of souls. Canon law is—and always has been—ordered toward the salvation of souls. The Church traditionally has expressed this truth through the Latin expression *"Salus animarum suprema lex"*—that is, "The salvation of souls is the supreme law." It is no coincidence that canon 1752, the code's closing canon, asks canonists and others who interpret canon law to remain ever mindful of this principle. Each law is formulated to further Christ's work of salvation.

It is our hope that we have faithfully explained the canons so that you can understand, appreciate and respect the supreme law of the Church. If the Holy Spirit uses these books to lead even one soul closer to heaven, we will consider our efforts worthwhile!

Glossary

Apostolic administrator: A cleric appointed by the Holy See to oversee an apostolic administration, such as a geographic area that is not a diocese or a diocese that has no bishop.

Apostolic Camera: A group of cardinals, presided over by the Cardinal Carmelengo (the Chancellor of the Apostolic Camera), that exercises special functions within the Holy See. One of these functions is to oversee the day-to-day operation of the Holy See when the papal office is vacant.

Apostolic Penitentiary: The branch of the Roman Curia that treats private matters, such as those raised in the confessional.

Archepiscopal Church: An Eastern Catholic Church overseen by a major archbishop who is not a patriarch.

Cardinal archpriest of the Vatican: The cardinal whom the pope appoints to coordinate liturgical matters in St. Peter's Basilica.

Cardinal vicar of Rome: The cardinal whom the pope entrusts with the care of the diocese of Rome on a day-to-day basis.

Carmelengo: The cardinal who presides over the Apostolic Camera. He is also called the Chancellor of the Apostolic Camera.

College of Bishops: The Roman Pontiff and the bishops in full communion with him.

College of Cardinals: The cardinals appointed by the Roman Pontiff.

College of consultors: A group of priests that a bishop selects from his council of priests for special responsibilities within the diocese.

Council of priests: Also known as the presbyteral council, a group of priests either elected by their fellow priests or appointed by the diocesan bishop to provide him with advice.

Dean of the College of Cardinals: The presider over the College of Cardinals. It is his responsibility to summon the papal conclave when a Roman Pontiff passes away or resigns from office.

Dicastery: An office of the Roman curia charged with overseeing a particular function. A dicastery is similar to a governmental department.

Diocesan administrator: The priest or auxiliary bishop who oversees the day-to-day operation of a diocese when there is no diocesan bishop due to death, transfer of office or resignation of the previous diocesan bishop.

Eparchy: A diocese of an Eastern Catholic Church in full communion with Rome.

Incardination: The binding of a cleric to a particular church (that is, diocese) or institute of consecrated life (that is, religious order).

Judicial vicar: A priest appointed by the diocesan bishop to oversee the diocese's judiciary.

Juridical person: A legal identity that is given to a group of Catholic faithful who have come together to form an official Catholic association or to an aspect of the Church's institution, such as a parish or a seminary. It is the Church's parallel to corporate status in civil law.

Postulator: A person responsible for advancing the cause of an individual toward canonization.

Prefect apostolic: A person appointed by the Holy See to oversee a territory where there is no Catholic diocese.

Promotor of justice or of the faith: An individual responsible for promoting the Church's law and discipline within the Church's internal legal system. The person would be akin to a prosecuting attorney in the civil legal system.

Pro-prefect apostolic: The person who temporarily acts in the place of the prefect apostolic.

Sui iuris: A term applied to an Eastern Catholic Church in full communion with Rome.

Tribunal: A Church court.

Vicar: One who is appointed to regularly act in the place of another. For example, the judicial vicar acts with the diocesan bishop on judicial matters, while the vicar general acts with the diocesan bishop when it comes to the exercise of executive power.

NOTES

Chapter One: Sacred Times and Places

1. *The 1917 or Pio-Benedictine Code of Canon Law* (San Francisco: Ignatius, 2001), canon 1165, paragraph 4.
2. *National Directory for the Formation, Ministry, and Life of Permanent Deacons in the United States* (Washington, D.C.: USCCB, 2005), no. 90.

Chapter Two: Holy Orders

1. For a discussion of validity and lawfulness, see *Surprised by Canon Law: 150 Questions Catholics Ask About Canon Law* (Cincinnati: Servant, 2004), pp. 7–9.

Chapter Four: Parish Life

1. For more on the council of priests, see *Surprised by Canon Law*, question 47, p. 40.
2. Congregation for Divine Worship and Discipline, *Omnia Ecclesia Titulum*, February 10, 1999, *Notitiae* 35 (1999), pp. 158–159.

Chapter Eight: The Canonization of Saints

1. Pope John Paul II, *Divinus Perfectionis Magister* (Divine Teacher and Model of Perfection), January 25, 1983, www.vatican.va.

Chapter Nine: The Election of a Pope

1. Pope John Paul II, Apostolic Letter *Motu Proprio, Ad Tuendam Fidem*, May 18, 1998, canon 1371, www.vatican.va.
2. Pope Benedict XVI, Apostolic Letter *Motu Proprio, De Alquibus Mutationibus in Normis de Eléctione Romani Pontificis*, June 11, 2007, www.vatican.va.

Chapter Eleven: Safeguarding the Sanctity of the Sacraments

1. See Charles J. Scicluna, "The Procedure and Praxis of the Congregation for the Doctrine of the Faith Regarding *Graviora Delicta*," in *Newsletter*, Canon Law Society of Great Britain and Ireland, Galashiels, Scotland, n. 139, September 2004, pp. 6–11.
2. Canadian Conference of Catholic Bishops, "From Pain to Hope," Ottawa, 1992, in Winter Report, Vol. II, p. A-20.
3. Address of John Paul II to cardinals of the United States, April 23, 2002, no. 3, www.vatican.va.
4. See Scicluna.

INDEX